THE POWER OF HUMILITY

THE POWER OF HUMILITY

R. T. KENDALL

Muddy
Pearl

UK edition published in 2013 by
Muddy Pearl, Edinburgh, Scotland.
www.muddypearl.com
books@muddypearl.com

First published by Charisma House Book Group. 600 Rinehart Road,
Lake Mary, Florida, 32746.
Copyright © R T Kendall 2011.
All rights reserved.
Available in other languages from Charisma Media, 600 Rinehart Road,
Lake Mary, FL 32746 charismahouse@charismamedia.com

British Library Cataloguing in Publication Data
A catalogue record for this book is available from the British Library

ISBN 978 1 910012 02 4

Typeset in Minion by Waverley Typesetters, Warham, Norfolk
Printed in Great Britain by Bell & Bain Ltd, Glasgow

To Greg and Christa, Logan and Alex

CONTENTS

FOREWORD

I am delighted – I can't use the word *proud* – to be asked to write the foreword to another book from the pen of my dear friend, Dr R. T. Kendall. With his usual courage and pastoral wisdom he has provided much-needed insight on a topic that is strangely and dangerously overlooked these days. Pride is a serious disease of the soul that all of us should be concerned about. Consider the following:

Pride is *deadly*. As pride takes root in our hearts, it slowly turns the focus of our lives away from God and towards self. We may sing, 'It's all about you, Jesus' but the reality is that it is now we who have become the focus of our worship. When this happens God withdraws His blessing from us. He has no option. For God to bless those who worship themselves would be for Him to reward idolatry.

Pride is *subtle*. Some sins, like some diseases, are obvious. You are unlikely to commit adultery, fall into a rage or forge a document without being aware of it. Pride, however, is very different and tiptoes unnoticed into the soul. In fact, it can enter our life accompanied by the very best of motives. So when we work hard to produce a good talk, play music well or prepare a fine meal, it is right and proper that we should be praised and accept that praise. Yet those merited compliments always bring with them the risk of pride: that we end up thinking more highly of ourselves than we should.

Pride is *universal*. No one can claim that they do not suffer from pride. Indeed, to claim you are free from pride is a sure sign that you are, in fact, proud, and an inflated self-image is a particular peril for those who are gifted and blessed by God. The higher you rise, the greater the peril of having your life fatally infected by pride.

Pride is *addictive*. Once you get to like the sound of being praised, you will seek ever more of it. Yet, like a drug, pride never delivers lasting satisfaction. You will soon find yourself resorting to ever more extreme measures to gain approval from others.

Pride is often *undetectable*. Pride can adopt an infinite number of disguises. The antidote to pride is humility. But there is false humility – well exposed by R.T. in these pages – which, while claiming to be the cure, in fact allows the disease to penetrate even deeper into the soul. Like some cunning virus, pride has a built-in mechanism to avoid detection. As R.T. points out, in one of his many discerning insights, we do not want to admit to our pride *because* of our pride!

Finally, pride *distorts* reality. Under the influence of pride, many sins can seem either attractive or necessary. So to boost our self-image we may resort to theft and adultery; to defend our reputation, we may lie and cheat. Pride withers our spiritual life. After all, when you are focused on loving yourself, it's very hard either to love your neighbour or your God. The result is spiritual fruitlessness and disaster. As the Bible wisely observes, 'Pride goes before destruction, a haughty spirit before a fall' (Proverbs 16:18).

Yet for all its seriousness, too little is said or spoken about pride today, even in the Christian world. Our culture certainly does not help. In the West we seem to have gone, within a generation, from treating pride as a sin to considering it one of life's essentials. We live in an age when it seems accepted that to succeed we must believe in ourselves, promote ourselves and assert ourselves. Our culture seems to be controlled by publicists, media consultants, public relations gurus and advisers on speech, dress and style. Pride has become legitimised: yesterday's vice has become today's virtue. In such a climate, it is hard to resist pride. Indeed, if you try to practise genuine humility you will soon have people telling you that you are committing career suicide. When everybody else is flying high on pride, publicity and self-promotion, to adopt a policy of modesty and humility seems like taking the slow train up a hill.

Pride is a particular challenge for Christians. We have a message to proclaim and a world that needs to hear it. We are under orders from our Master not to retreat from involvement with those around us. Yet how, in a world obsessed by advertising and self-promotion, can we proclaim the good news without putting ourselves before Christ? How can we promote the message without the spotlight hurting the messenger? We need to do some hard and biblical thinking.

Given the perils of pride, it is perhaps surprising that so few people have written about it. Yet it is a dangerous and difficult topic: if nothing else, there would be a terrible irony in coming to believe that you had written a really good book about pride. The reality is that it is precisely someone like Dr R. T. Kendall, who has been at the top and who now has nothing to prove and nothing to lose, who can best talk about pride.

So I am very grateful for this profoundly stimulating, challenging and provocative book. It is stamped throughout with the heartfelt honesty, spiritual insight and biblical knowledge that have long been the valued trademarks of R. T. Kendall. R.T. defines pride as 'taking yourself too seriously'. In this book he certainly doesn't take himself seriously. But he does take God, His Word and the dangers of pride seriously – and that is exactly what we need to hear.

REVEREND CANON J. JOHN

INTRODUCTION

Writing a book on pride is ominously close to authoring a book called 'Humility – and how I attained it'. But I must begin with a revealing anecdote.

After my publisher and I agreed on this book – a follow-up to *The Sin No One Talks About – Jealousy,* they asked me to present them with an outline before moving forward. I was not happy. 'What?' I retorted. 'Are you making me jump through hoops as if I were a novice author after all the books I have done with you? Why do I have to prove myself like this?' They explained that with the present economy being as it is, they had to adopt this procedure and they hoped I would comply. I refused.

I am ashamed to say I had not initially realised the irony of this. Here we were discussing a book on *pride*. It was my pride that might have aborted the production of this very book. I began to see how my pride was becoming more important than the book we were contemplating. I came to my senses and immediately sent in an outline for the book you are now reading. I was embarrassingly found out in the embryonic stage of this new book, a matter which my publisher quickly noticed – but was graciously prepared to overlook.

Caution: you are about to read a book by an imperfect author. If you think that I have won a big victory over pride, one which qualifies me to write this book, you could not be more wrong. And yet this disclosure of my own weakness in this area reminded me how pervasive the matter of pride is. I am admitting to 'the sin no one admits to', yes, but it is easier to do this when you are writing a book on it. It is not necessarily a sign of humility.

Why do we not want to admit to our pride? It is because of our pride! There are always exceptions of course, but generally speaking we are loath to reveal the *real* reason that lies behind many of our decisions. Pride is usually the true explanation why our feelings are hurt, why we hate being passed over for the wonderful invitation, why we feel rejection, why we get into trouble, why we won't admit to a mistake, why we want to be seen with certain people, why we are afraid we won't get credit for what we did, why we *stay* angry and, yes, why we are jealous. Pride is at the bottom of envy and jealousy. Pride and jealousy are first cousins within this dysfunctional family called the human race.

The purpose of my book is two-fold. First, it is to help us see more deeply into our hearts and motives. 'The heart is deceitful above all things and beyond cure. Who can understand it?' (Jeremiah 17:9). For this reason we only arrive at self-knowledge in increments – and never totally get there in this life. But seeing ourselves – embarrassing though it can be – may hopefully drive us to want to improve.

Therefore secondly, and mainly – and I pray this for every reader – it is that you will be motivated to be more like Jesus. Jesus was perfect. He was the God-man. He never sinned. He was tempted by all the things that tempt you and me, but, unlike us, He never gave in (Hebrews 4:15). Jesus did not have pride in the sense that the Bible uses that word. To put it another way: Jesus was never *proud*, that is, He was never – ever – conceited, smug or arrogant. You and I will never be completely like Jesus until we are glorified (Romans 8:30; 1 John 3:2). But we can begin now to emulate Him as much as possible.

We will see below that having pride is not always and necessarily a sin, and yet the Bible never has a single good thing to say about it. It is always listed with the worst of sins – '... sexual immorality, theft, murder, adultery, coveting, wickedness, deceit, sensuality, envy, slander, *pride* ...' (Mark 7:21–22 ESV). In the last days, says

Paul, 'people will be lovers of themselves, lovers of money, boastful, *proud ...'* (2 Timothy 3:2).

I write books to change lives. May God grant this to be true with the book you now hold in your hands.

1

TAKING OURSELVES TOO
SERIOUSLY

*'"I am the only one of the Lord's prophets left,...I have been very
zealous for the Lord God Almighty."'*
  I Kings 18:22; 19:14

*'There is no limit to how far a person can go, as long as he doesn't
care who gets the credit for it.'*
  Plaque on President Ronald Reagan's desk

A measure of pride is essential to our self-esteem,
emotional well being and good mental health. It is what
gives us a sense of self-worth and dignity – which God
wants each of us to have. We need to take ourselves seriously to
some extent. But pride can push this too far when we begin to
take ourselves too seriously. In Chapter 2 we will look at
the good side of pride – its advantages to us and why it is not
always bad. In this chapter however we will examine pride
as it is generally understood in the Bible. As I said above, the
Bible has nothing good to say about pride. Pride in Scripture is
always that which is suspect and to be avoided; it is disdained.
It is assumed in the Bible as arrogance, haughtiness, smugness,
a feeling of superiority over others, insolence, overbearingness,
superciliousness, narcissism, vainglory, conceit, egotism, vanity,
self-importance.

Pride is the opposite of humility, modesty and meekness. St Augustine (d. AD 430) said that pride is 'the love of one's own excellence'. People like Aristotle (384–322 BC) and George Bernard Shaw (1856–1950) saw pride as a profound virtue. 'I often quote myself', said Shaw, 'it adds spice to my conversation.' 'Few people think more than two or three times a year', he said. 'I have made an international reputation for myself by thinking once or twice a week.'

Most religions of the world – certainly Christianity – see pride as a sin. There are two Greek words relevant here. *Alazon* (as in James 4:16; 1 John 2:16; Romans 1:30) refers to one who makes more of himself than reality justifies, ascribing to himself either more or better things than he has, or even what he does not possess at all; he promises what he cannot deliver. The other Greek word is *hyperephanos* (as in Mark 7:22, James 4:6, 1 Peter 5:5) which means arrogance. It refers to one who brags about his position, power and wealth and despises others. In 2 Timothy 3:2 both *alazon* (boastful) and *hyperephanos* (proud) are found beside each other.

Elijah

We will see throughout this book that neither word for 'pride' need be used explicitly to describe a person's proud behaviour. For example, the writer of 1 Kings did not impute Elijah with pride. But that is what was going on. How dare Elijah say, 'I am the only one of the Lord's prophets left' (1 Kings 18:22; 19:14) – even if it were true! But it was absolutely false. Elijah had just been told that Obadiah the prophet had taken a hundred other prophets and hid them in caves (1 Kings 18:13). Elijah felt so superior to the other prophets of his day that he did not even acknowledge them as prophets of the Lord! That is sheer arrogance. Elijah is a perfect example of a person taking himself too seriously.

Could the revered and hallowed Elijah truly take himself too seriously? Yes. Is not Elijah regarded as one of the greatest men in the Old Testament? Yes. Did his prayer before all the people not result in fire coming down from heaven and exposing the folly of the prophets of Baal? Yes. Was it not Elijah who appeared with Moses when Jesus was transfigured before the disciples on the mountain (Matthew 17:3)? Yes. And when Elijah said, 'I am the only one of the Lord's prophets left', God could have aborted the whole procedure because Elijah misspoke (to put it mildly). But God didn't do that.

This encourages me. James wanted his readers to know that Elijah was 'a man with a nature like ours' (James 5:17 ESV). The point is, if God could use Elijah – and if Elijah can get his prayers answered, so too with any of us! God can use those of us who take ourselves too seriously. In the final chapter of my book *In Pursuit of His Glory* I listed five things I would hopefully do differently if I could turn the clock back after twenty-five years at Westminster Chapel. This included that I should not take myself so seriously.

I therefore define pride essentially as taking oneself too seriously. Taking oneself too seriously is the common denominator in all proud people. It describes those who resent criticism, who are insecure, who cannot laugh at themselves, whose need of praise is constant, who see themselves as overly important, who fancy themselves as being very special to God (and think God bends the rules for them), who tend to blame others for their problems, who hate taking the blame, who cannot bear not getting the credit for the good they did and who have an insatiable need to prove themselves.

Is that you? Take heart. I just described virtually every person that God has ever used.

Categories of pride

But pride takes many forms. Some try to prove they are *not* proud by trying to appear the very opposite. 'Pride perceiving humility honourable, often borrows her cloak', said Benjamin Franklin (1706–1790). It goes down better with people if we seem humble. The motive is the same: we are concerned how we are perceived. Our self-esteem is at stake.

There are many kinds of pride. There is social pride (keeping up with the Joneses), spiritual pride (self-righteousness), financial pride (impressing others with one's wealth), political pride (being sure to be politically correct), sexual pride (always needing to attract the opposite sex), cultural pride (impressing people with your love of the arts), pride of pedigree (placing importance on one's background), educational pride (impressing with degrees), intellectual pride (always needing to prove how much you know and how intelligent you are), pride of your good looks (overly concerned with appearance, whether regarding dress, figure or hair), national pride (sometimes being overly patriotic) or racial pride (proud of the colour of your skin). There is even theological pride, when someone feels superior because of their rightness of doctrine. Closely akin to this is prophetic pride, when someone gloats over their prophetic successes.

God hates a proud look

What must never be forgotten is that *God hates pride*. 'There are six things the Lord hates, seven that are detestable to him: haughty eyes (a proud look, KJV), a lying tongue, hands that shed innocent blood, a heart that devises wicked schemes, feet that are quick to rush into evil, a false witness who pours out lies and a man who stirs up dissension among brothers' (Proverbs 6:16–19). Note that 'haughty eyes' or 'proud look' heads the list of things God hates. 'Whoever has haughty eyes and a proud heart, him will I not endure' (Psalms 101:5). Have you ever seen anyone with a proud look or haughty eyes? I have. Certain people literally come to my mind when I think of haughty eyes and an arrogant countenance. But who am I to judge? You and I look on the outward appearance; God looks at the heart (1 Samuel 16:7). So have I too had the same outward proud expression I have seen in some when in fact people have had the exact same perception of me? I don't think I want the answer to that question.

When we consider how much God *hates* our being proud it is enough to drive us to our knees. We should ask, 'Lord, am I like this?' 'You save the humble but bring low those whose eyes are haughty' (Psalms 18:27). 'God opposes the proud but gives grace to the humble' (1 Peter 5:5). 'Everyone who exalts himself will be humbled' (Luke 14:11). 'You rebuke the arrogant' (Psalms 119:21).

But when I consider that God was patient with Elijah, I feel there is hope for me. God could indeed have stepped in and interrupted the entire proceedings when Elijah openly said, 'I am the only true prophet left'. But He didn't. God took His time and later on called Elijah to one side, as if to say, 'Oh by the way Elijah, I have seven thousand in Israel whose knees have not bowed down to Baal' (see 1 Kings 19:18). God has used me over the years and then later called me to one side and gently showed me faults and flaws others saw but I had been blind to. He is such a good and gracious God.

No guilt trip

I will have failed in this book if I give you a guilt trip as you read. My task is to show our pride and God's hatred of it – but to show we are all in this together. But more than that, that we will equally see His mercy toward those who repent of this folly. The worst thing you and I can do in this connection is to be defensive. That will never do. But if God kindly points out our failures it means we are loved (1 John 4:19) – and that there is hope for us. Repentance is a grace that God *grants* (Romans 2:4; Acts 11:48; 2 Timothy 2:25). It is a gracious gift which we do not remotely deserve. The very real possibility of being unable to be renewed to repentance (Hebrews 6:4–6) should be enough to humble all of us. But if in this book you are given to see what displeases the Lord and that you are sorry, I will give God the praise.

Even Ahab, one of the most wicked kings ever, saw his folly in a most heinous injustice he committed. But when he was reproved, he 'tore his clothes, put on sackcloth and fasted. He lay in sackcloth and went around meekly'. God noticed it. He said to Elijah, '"Have you noticed how Ahab has humbled himself before me? Because he has humbled himself, I will not bring this disaster in his day, but I will bring it on his house in the days of his son"' (1 Kings 21:27–29). This means there is hope for us all.

God rebukes us to bring us to our senses. He lets us save face. He does not chasten or discipline us to 'get even'. God got even at the cross, when 'the Lord . . . laid on [Jesus] the iniquity of us all' (Isaiah 53:6). 'For as high as the heavens are above the earth, so great is his love for those who fear him; as far as the east is from the west, so far has he removed our transgressions from us. As a father has compassion on his children, so the Lord has compassion on those who fear him; for he knows how we are formed, he remembers that we are dust' (Psalms 103:11–14). He sent the wind and the fish to swallow up Jonah, not to punish him but, as Dr Bruce Chesser put it, to save him (Jonah 1–2). How often God 'saves us from ourselves', as Dr Martyn Lloyd-Jones used to say.

Foolish worry: what people might think of us

Taking ourselves too seriously leads us foolishly to imagine what people might think about us. As if what they think is so important! But I will never forget a day – it was pivotal in my life – when two important men had to humble me. These two men were Dr Barrie White, my supervisor at Oxford, and Dr J. I. Packer, who functioned as a second supervisor. I had been at Oxford for about a year at the time. What I thought was to be a leisurely lunch with them was interrupted by Jim Packer saying to Barrie White, 'Shall you tell him or shall I?' Dr White motioned to Dr Packer to start. 'You need to minimise your liabilities', Jim Packer graciously said to me, showing a mastery of British understatement – and trying to let me save face. 'I know you have come to Oxford to do your D.Phil. on John Owen'. (He was referring to the great Puritan theologian John Owen (1616–1683) whose doctrine of the priestly work of Christ had motivated me to come to Oxford, something I had told everybody back in America I would do.) Jim continued, 'But we don't think you are able to do John Owen', then shared what they thought I *could* do at Oxford to get the D.Phil.

I was devastated. I went home with the worst migraine headache of my whole life. I went to bed. Why? *I worried what people would think.* It was so silly. The truth is, these people would have thought absolutely nothing about it! But I could only think of my reputation among friends back in America. Taking myself too seriously literally put me to bed. What is more: the thesis I ended up doing (on John Calvin (1509–1564)] and the English Puritans) was the best thing in that connection that ever happened to me. But at the time I was utterly governed by pride and what people would think, that friends back at my Seminary in Louisville might discover I wasn't cut out to do a doctorate on John Owen. And yet it reminds me of something my grandfather R. J. Kendall used to say: 'Don't worry over what people might be thinking of you; chances are, they are not thinking about you at all.' How true.

Building monuments to ourselves

Taking oneself too seriously is what makes people try to ensure they will be remembered by history. They have statues made, get buildings, streets or highways named after them *while they are still alive.* The notion to 'Let another praise you, and not your own mouth; someone else, and not your own lips' (Proverbs 27:2) seems not to appear on their radar screen. And yet it reminds me of something President Harry S. Truman (1884–1972) would say when refusing to let anybody sculpt a bust or statue of him. He said, 'I don't want people seeing my statue years later and asking, "Who was he?"'

I was disappointed when one of my heroes allowed a larger-than-life statue to be made of himself by America's greatest sculptor while he was still alive – and was even present for its unveiling! It's true! They had planned to put the statue outside in the open air. But the preacher stopped them. 'No, please put it inside. I don't want those pigeons defecating on my statue.' But here is something I think is rather funny. I decided sometime later to use this account as an illustration in a sermon, realising nobody in the congregation at Westminster would remotely twig who I was talking about. My point in the sermon – on rewards – was that God might have to say to this great preacher at the Judgment Seat of Christ, 'Sorry, my son, there is no reward laid up for you now, you got it all below with that statue you let them make of you.' So far, so good. But I was shocked to learn afterwards that at least six people were present from this man's church! By the way, he was a great man indeed. Now in heaven, if anyone deserved a statue, he did. But after he was gone.

Those in Scripture who built monuments to themselves while they were alive however were tragic figures. I have always been gripped by this. In fact there are two accounts in this connection that have deeply shaped my thinking. First, King Saul had a monument built to himself while he was still alive (1 Samuel 15:12). He had already become yesterday's man when this happened. Second, years later Absalom stole the hearts of the people and forced his father King David to live in exile for a while. David was later restored to the kingship and will always be regarded as Israel's greatest king. As for Absalom, 'during his lifetime' he took 'a pillar and erected it in the King's Valley as a monument to himself, for he thought, 'I have no son to carry on the memory of my name.' He named the pillar after himself, and it is called Absalom's Monument to this day' (2 Samuel 18:18).

What matters most of all

There is one thing – and one thing alone – that ultimately matters: God's opinion of you and me. If His opinion doesn't matter to you now, it will then. This opinion will be openly revealed at the Judgment Seat of Christ. You then will learn what God thinks of you. And you will see what He thinks of me. I can safely promise you that any accolade, humiliation, monument, criticism, put-down, compliment, praise, disappointment, lie, statue, honour or prize here on this earth will mean *nothing* then. Nothing. Except *how we handled* such things – which will largely determine what God thinks of us. Why therefore should we ever want the praise of people here below? Why should it mean so much to us? I will come clean with you: I love compliments. A close friend (who knows me well) had a tee-shirt made for my birthday that says 'Compliments are in order'. But the thought of pre-empting what God himself might say to me on the Day – by amassing all the awards and compliments I can get below – scares me to death. I propose to live for that Day – seeking no honour or praise but His.

The irony is, if the plaque on Ronald Reagan's desk is correct – that *there is no limit to how far a person can go, as long as he doesn't care who gets to the credit for it*, we will accomplish more than ever in this life if we don't take ourselves so seriously! The way up is down. '... he who humbles himself will be exalted' (Luke 14:11). 'Humble yourselves, therefore, under the mighty hand of God so that at the proper time he may exalt you' (1 Peter 5:6 ESV).

John speaks of worldliness as 'the boasting of what [man] has and does'. The KJV calls it 'the pride of life', the ESV footnote calls it 'pride in possessions' (1 John 2:16). It refers to our effort to impress people with what we have accumulated. This could refer to material things, achievements, awards, antiques, pottery, photographs with important people, prestigious jobs, degrees, clothes, furniture, art, carpet, cars, framed commendations or letters – all there to impress you! I fear there are people for whom these things matter more than anything in the world. How sad. I remember going to a home of some people in Rome many years ago. The main reason they wanted me to come to their home was to see their apartment and collection of bone china. It truly was impressive. But this was all they apparently had to bolster their self-esteem. It was as though their apartment and china gave people warrant to take them seriously. They seemed to feel I would take them truly seriously if I saw these possessions. It was all they lived for – to invite people to see their apartment and china collection.

We who are Christians sometimes forget we are going to heaven one day – and will be there a long time! Have you ever pondered the depth of these famous lines?

'When we've been there ten thousand years,
Bright shining as the sun;
We've no less days to sing God's praise
Than when we first begun.'

John Newton (1725–1807)

Think about this. After we have been in heaven for ten thousand years it will be like the first day. Do we really believe this? I do. Why ever do we live in this present world as though this present existence is all there is? It seems to me that the thought of going to heaven one day – to be there forever – should help us on our way not to take circumstances here below – or ourselves – so seriously.

2

IS PRIDE ALWAYS A BAD THING?

'"When someone invites you to a wedding feast, do not take the place of honour, for a person more distinguished than you may have been invited. If so, the host who invited both of you will come and say to you, 'Give this man your seat'. Then, humiliated, you will have to take the least important place. But when you are invited, take the lowest place, so that when your host comes, he will say to you, 'Friend, move up to a better place'. Then you will be honoured in the presence of all your fellow guests. For everyone who exalts himself will be humbled, and he who humbles himself will be exalted."'

Luke 14:8–11

'There is this paradox in pride – it makes some men ridiculous, but prevents others from becoming so.'

Samuel Taylor Coleridge (1772–1800)

'Disciplining yourself to do what you know is right and important, although difficult, is the high road to pride, self-esteem and personal satisfaction.'

Margaret Thatcher (1925–2013)

Although the Bible has nothing good to say about pride, Jesus' parable about our taking the 'lowest seat' at a banquet is a direct appeal to our pride. This shows that pride can be a good thing. Jesus assumes this. He does not want us to be 'humiliated' but 'honoured' – but only when we go about it the right way.

There is no virtue in being humiliated because of pride getting in the way, but there certainly is virtue in being humble in order to be honoured God's way. The latter comes by not letting pride get in the way. Jesus therefore appeals to our pride in order to protect us from unnecessary humiliation. He also shows that it is good in his sight to be honoured when we have arrived at this honour by being humble.

This is why Peter said that we should 'Humble yourselves, therefore, under the mighty hand of God so that at the proper time he may exalt you' (1 Peter 5:6 ESV). God is not jealous of our being exalted if He in fact is the one behind it. He promises to get on our case and exalt us when we truly humble ourselves. But if we exalt ourselves, He works as our enemy.

Our pre-fallen state

We must never overlook or take for granted that our first parents – Adam and Eve – were created in the Garden of Eden without sin (Genesis 2). It is easy to forget this. You and I were born into this world *not* as Adam and Eve were originally created but as fallen creatures. Once they sinned – which is called the Fall – everything changed. As a result of the Fall, we inherited Adam's nature when we were born – known as original sin. We all were conceived in sin (see Psalm 51:5). We were consequently born with a propensity to sin. We came from our mother's womb with a sinful nature. 'Even from birth the wicked go astray; from the womb they are wayward and speak lies' (Psalm 58:3). This is why you don't need to teach a child to lie. You do have to teach him or her to tell the truth.

All theology and anthropology must therefore be carried out in the light of mankind before the Fall and after the Fall. St Augustine referred to the four stages of mankind: (1) man before the Fall – *able to sin*; (2) man after the Fall – *not able not to sin*; (3) man after regeneration (born again) – *able not to sin*; (4)

mankind after glorification (when we are in heaven) – *not able to sin.*

Man in his pre-fallen state was, among other things, made for affirmation, affection and attention. That was true in our pre-fallen state, and it is still true with all of us today. Sin warps our need for these things – resulting in our craving and seeking unwarranted affirmation, inappropriate affection and inordinate attention.

God made us 'subject to vanity' (kjv), 'subjected to futility' (esv), 'subjected to frustration' (niv) (Romans 8:20). We were created in the Garden of Eden before the Fall with an innate sense of self-esteem and dignity. After all, we were created in God's own image (Genesis 1:26). One might call it unfallen pride – in Adam and Eve before the Fall. But a question follows: what happened to this pride now that you and I are born with original sin? Answer: the image of God in us has *not* been totally obliterated. This means that despite inheriting the sin of Adam, there is still a certain self-esteem and dignity we are born with which is not necessarily sinful although subject to sin. It is our duty to keep this under control. But we all fail (see Romans 3:23). But the degree to which it is kept under control (by the Holy Spirit) will be the degree to which our pride can be used for the glory of God.

Where pride is good

It is pride that makes us want to better ourselves. It is what motivates us to look presentable in public. It is a sense of dignity that makes us want to comb our hair, brush our teeth, bathe ourselves, shine our shoes and wear nice clothes. When we lose that dignity we lose any care of ourselves – like some of those who live in the streets. Living without regard to our appearance would please the devil and certainly does not bring glory to God.

I knew a man in London who was once doing missionary work in Africa. Things went wrong while he was there and he got mixed up with a cult called the Children of God back in the 1970s. He apparently became venal, profligate and bitter toward the church. He moved back to London. He would come to

13

Westminster Chapel but only to mix with people after the services with the view to distorting all I preached. We finally had to forbid his coming inside the doors of the church. So he now walks back and forth in front of the chapel with his posters warning people against us. He is unkempt, wears dirty clothes, looks very strange and is probably demon-possessed. He has lost all sense of personal dignity. His very appearance scares people off – which is what he wants in order to keep people away from Westminster Chapel.

The loss of self-esteem and dignity therefore is as dishonouring to God as is 'the cravings of sinful man, the lust of his eyes and the boasting of what he has and does' (1 John 2:16). The devil would have us go from one extreme to the other. The way I would put it is this. We should want to call forth that pre-fallen pride in us – which Adam had before the Fall. This is the way we should live. This pride can help us avoid the pitfall of becoming proud.

An irony is, by showing proper self-respect we can end up with the open praise and admiration we may have wanted all along. For example, Jesus gives us the way to exaltation: take the lowest seat. That is the principle. Whether it be an invitation to a banquet or opportunity to minister, we should not aim for the limelight – but the opposite. If we aim for the limelight – the top table as it were, we will likely be humiliated. But if we aim for the lowest seat (we have nothing to lose) we may well be exalted.

You could call it shrewd humility. Staying humble is playing it safe. It keeps you from embarrassment. If you don't get exalted you are still in a good place. We are not to aim for exaltation anyway! But humbling ourselves is always the right move and, just maybe, along the way we will be beckoned to move upward. And yet it is our *good* pride – pre-fallen pride – that keeps us from looking ridiculous. This is what Samuel Taylor Coleridge meant when he said, 'There is a paradox in pride – it makes some men ridiculous (like taking the highest seat of honour only to be humiliated), but prevents others from becoming so' (having the good sense to take the lowest seat and not be humiliated).

An analogy

This 'good' pride may be compared to good cholesterol. Cholesterol is a substance in the blood that promotes arteriosclerosis – which can lead to serious heart problems. But there is good cholesterol and there is bad cholesterol in us – we all have both. The bad is what is injurious to our health. A sensible diet and proper exercise can stem the tide away from bad cholesterol and keep our cholesterol generally more like it should be. The bad cholesterol, then, is like the arrogance, boastfulness, conceit and all that is unattractive about us and which inevitably gets us into trouble. We therefore must never dismiss the importance of good pride and dignity in our lives as Christians.

But there is 'good' pride in other areas of our lives. Someone has said, 'Pride is a personal commitment. It is an attitude which separates excellence from mediocrity'. The good pride is what propels us to excel. Martin Luther (1483–1547) said that God uses sex to drive a man to marriage, ambition to drive a man to service and fear to drive a man to faith. Ambition therefore is a God-given proponent that should be respected and honoured as long as it does not get out of control. My own father drove me to get good grades in school. This drivenness has been a part of my motivation all my life. The good side is that I did so well academically at my Seminary they recommended me for Oxford. The bad side is that I neglected my family during the time I was at Westminster Chapel – driven to preach good sermons. Whereas the sermons may have been a blessing to some, my preoccupation with excellence became a curse in other ways. If I had the choice to relive those years I would choose time with family a hundred times over time in preparation of sermons.

Common grace

Pride, then, when it is like good cholesterol in the body, can be a blessing to the world. There is a Japanese proverb, 'It is a beggar's pride that he is not a thief'. That spark of pride – which might keep a desperate man from committing a crime – should be appreciated and affirmed. Thank God for it. This is part of the self-respect, dignity and honour with which a man and a woman were endowed at creation. It is also called *conscience*, an innate sense of right and wrong in every person – endowed by the Creator (Romans 1:19–20; 2:15). Every person on the planet has a conscience – a gift of God.

To put it another way, good pride is part of 'common grace'. John Calvin taught that there is a 'special grace in nature', meaning that there is something good in all men – *saved and lost*. There are two levels of grace: (1) *common* grace (God's goodness given in measure to all – saved or lost) and (2) *saving* grace (God's salvation given only to believers). It is called 'common grace' not because it is ordinary but because it is given in varying degrees *commonly* to all people. Common grace, then, is not saving grace. Saving grace is the sovereign work of the Holy Spirit, showing us that we are sinners and that Jesus died for us and rose from the dead. Faith alone in Jesus Christ is what fits us for heaven. To put it another way, all believers have a measure of common grace but not all who have common grace have saving grace.

Common grace is what you and I were born with prior to conversion. It is the explanation for our level of intelligence, our talents, our interests, our motivation and our desire to better ourselves. It is what gives one a love for music, literature or science. Keep in mind that it has nothing to do with salvation. But it is a wonderful part of our being human beings. It is also the reason for the 'good' pride in people – whether or not they are saved.

The good pride in people is what makes people want to excel. It is what motivates some to become doctors, teachers, nurses, engineers. It is the reason the world is not utterly topsy-turvy. It is the reason we have law, hospitals, piano concertos, musicians, scientific achievements, highways, policemen, firemen, men and women in the military and inventions that help all humankind.

That is not all; there is a spark of human kindness in nature that gives people an urge to help the hurting. This is what lies behind the Good Samaritans of this world. In a parable Jesus talked about a man who, unlike religious people, came to the aid of a man who had fallen into the hands of robbers. The Samaritan took pity on him, bandaged his wounds, pouring on oil and wine. 'Then he put the man on his own donkey, took him to an inn and took care of him' – and looked after his financial needs as well (Luke 10:25–37). Have you wondered what makes people like this? It is God's common grace. We have just come through a flood here in the Nashville area – the worst, they say, in a hundred years. The stories of those who volunteered to help the helpless who lost their homes and possessions are amazing. What makes people do good things like this is not necessarily because they are saved – they may not be saved at all – but because they want to help people. It is a part of God's common grace.

There is in every human being a spark of goodness. This 'good cholesterol' is what can motivate people to do extraordinary things. However, this too must be put into perspective: 'I saw that all labour and all achievement spring from man's envy of his neighbour' (Ecclesiastes 4:4). The desire to make others envious is partly what lies behind great music of this world, Nobel prizes and extraordinary accomplishments.

It is because of the Fall, then, that sin came into the world and the reason we have a perverted nature. But in spite of this there is 'special grace in nature' which may benefit everybody. And yet the depravity in us is what lets the 'bad cholesterol' get the upper hand. For example, pride becomes arrogance, dignity becomes smugness, self-respect becomes insolence, the desire for affirmation becomes an insatiable ego trip, the desire for affection becomes sexual promiscuity and the desire for attention becomes sheer self-love.

Crossing over a line – from dignity to arrogance

It is not always easy to judge at what point one crosses over a line – when self-respect turns into carnal pride. I only know that we all need to be on guard against taking ourselves too seriously. This is partly what is meant by 'Keep thy heart with all diligence' (Proverbs 4:23 KJV). But if we can avoid taking ourselves too seriously while maintaining a sense of self-worth at the same time we should be truly thankful. The goal then is to maintain sufficient self-respect and personal dignity without becoming proud. This way we do not let our Heavenly Father down.

Therefore be thankful for a measure of common grace that makes you want to better yourself, to get to work on time, help the hurting, be the best employee in the company, excel when it comes to integrity and outdo those around you in excellence and hard work. But we must do these things without gloating or becoming smug. The parallel benefit from avoiding arrogance is that you can maintain a good conscience and bring great honour to God.

Common grace in the Christian

Whereas common grace in a non-Christian can produce a Shakespeare, an Einstein or a Mozart, what about the measure of common grace in the believer? Not all non-Christians are scientists or composers of great music. They are in fact few. This is true also with special common grace in the believer. Most of us are very ordinary. 'For consider your calling, brothers: not many of you were wise according to worldly standards, not many were powerful, not many were of noble birth' (1 Corinthians 1:26 ESV). But now and then God endows some Christians with unusual natural ability. When a great measure of special grace in nature *plus* saving grace come along, you have the explanation for the Apostle Pauls of this world, the St Augustines, the Thomas Aquinases, the Anselms, the Jonathan Edwardses – those rare minds that show how the Christian faith can stand up to any intellectual challenge.

However, those who are highly gifted in the church are going to be judged more strictly. '"From everyone who has been given much, much will be demanded; and from the one who has been entrusted with much, much more will be asked"' (Luke 12:48). Whereas God may use pride or ambition to motivate to service, we must beware lest our pride cross over a line and become vanity. No matter how much we may accomplish we must disdain all pride in us and confess openly before God, '" 'We are unworthy servants; we have only done our duty'"' (Luke 17:10).

The worst thing that can happen to us in this connection is to begin to feel proud, supposing that we are special or unique – and that we should be awarded for our efforts. God may well reward us – for he has promised to do so, but when we think we have earned it we simultaneously cross over the line and show the very arrogance that displeases God.

What is the way forward? It is to let a sense of duty propel us to service but 'not let your left hand know what your right hand is doing' (Matthew 6:3). As John Stott put it, there is a sense in which we 'do not even tell ourselves' what we might have done for God – lest pride worm its way into our deceitful hearts.

I promise you: the moment the good pride crosses over a line and becomes bad pride, your soul will suffer. Therefore do not ever trust the good pride, only thank God for a particular level of gifting and motivation that enables you to excel. Remember Paul's searching questions: 'For who makes you different from anyone else? What do you have that you did not receive? And if you did receive it, why do you boast as though you did not?' (1 Corinthians 4:7). The moment you began to take yourself too seriously was precisely when you crossed over the line.

3

THE HIGH COST OF PRIDE

' "My little finger is thicker than my father's waist. My father laid on you a heavy yoke; I will make it even heavier. My father scourged you with whips; I will scourge you with scorpions." '

1 Kings 12:10–11

'I have been more and more convinced, the more I think of it, that, in general, pride is at the bottom of all great mistakes. All other passions do occasional good; but whenever pride puts in its word, everything goes wrong; and what it might really be desirable to do, quiet and innocently, it is normally dangerous to do proudly.'

John Ruskin (1819–1900)

Pause for a moment and consider a mistake you have made in your life. Try to be honest. Perhaps there is more than one mistake you have made. Have you ever asked whether it was *pride* that lay at the bottom of these mistakes?

The purpose of this chapter is to help us face our pride – past and present, then ask whether we might avoid a future mistake by catching ourselves in the nick of time. But it is not easy to do. Pride is the sin we are loath to admit to.

Some readers may recall that I am a graduate of Trevecca Nazarene University in Nashville, Tennessee. But I did my Trevecca stint in two stages. The first was from 1953–1956. During that time I felt a call to preach and became a Nazarene pastor in Palmer, Tennessee while still a student. I was given a new Chevrolet by my grandmother to drive to Palmer on weekends. I had a 'Damascus road' experience driving in my car on 31 October 1955 and immediately underwent a radical theological change. I resigned my church in Palmer in May 1956 and became fairly sure that my future would not be in my old denomination. I left Trevecca before I finished my Bachelor of Arts degree. It is highly debatable whether leaving Trevecca in 1956 was a good decision.

I returned to my home town of Ashland, Kentucky in 1956. I had to get a job. I also had to buy a car since my grandmother who gave me the Chevrolet understandably took it back. I worked as a salesman by knocking on doors. I began to make a little money for the first time in my life but was immature in handling money. I sadly developed a taste for material things. I went deep into debt by buying expensive clothes, very nice shoes, took airplane lessons and even purchased my own airplane. I rationalised that in my future ministry I would need an airplane! I later bought a new car – a 1957 Edsel. I was several thousands of dollars in debt and in no position to be in Christian ministry. It was approximately six years before I was out of debt. Although I have never regretted marrying Louise (in 1958), we should have waited until my bills were paid.

My pride was at the bottom of my indebtedness and love for material things. Even though *all* that happened eventually worked together for my good (Romans 8:28) and I truly learned how to handle money (I have never been in debt since), here were six wasted years in my youth that might have been used completely for further preparation and ministry. I swallowed my pride over leaving Trevecca prematurely and returned there in 1970 to finish my A.B. degree.

Six wasted years. That was a pretty high cost if you ask me. It is humbling to admit to a mistake – whether or not pride was the reason for that mistake. I don't think pride is necessarily the only reason for all mistakes we make, but almost certainly it is the cause for many if not most of them.

The cost of pride is evident so often in time lost, energy wasted, money misused, losing friends, forfeiting wisdom, opportunities blown away, embarrassment, how one deals with their enemy, wanting to upstage a rival, overestimating one's own gift, not living within the limits of one's particular calling or anointing, not listening to advice or seeking a second opinion, not listening to God, not confessing sin and refusing to admit to mistakes.

It is often said that we men don't like to take instructions if we are lost when driving. I'm afraid in my case it is true. I will never forget driving into east London (always a nightmare) to an address we hadn't been to before. Louise tried to persuade me to ask someone where we were once we were lost. 'No', I firmly replied, 'I know where we are and where we are going'. Wrong. An hour later (after an hour wasted), having finally listened to advice, we reached our destination. The cost of pride. Even if that story was a drop in the bucket compared to examples below.

Pharaoh

The Lord ordered Pharaoh, through Moses '"'Let my people go, so that they may hold a festival to [me] in the desert.'" Pharaoh said, "Who is the Lord, that I should obey him and let Israel go? I do not know the Lord and I will not let Israel go"' (Exodus 5:1–2). God sent one plague after another. At times it seemed that Pharaoh caved in, but would later relent. The tenth plague was God destroying of all the firstborn in Egypt. Only those who were covered by the blood of the sacrificial lamb were spared (see Exodus 12:13). This meant that even Pharaoh's own firstborn son died (Exodus 12:29). At this he finally said, '"Up! Leave my people, you and the Israelites! Go, worship the Lord as you have requested"' (Exodus 12:31). But after the children of Israel left, Pharaoh's stubborn pride set in yet again and he decided to chase them. He took his army and ordered six hundred of his best chariots, along with all the other chariots of Egypt, with officers over all of them.

Whereas the Lord hardening Pharaoh's heart is the divine explanation for Pharaoh's irrational decision (see Exodus 14:8), his pride is the human explanation; his stature before all Egypt was at stake. As a consequence, the Egyptians pursued the Israelites into the Red Sea while the waters were being supernaturally held back. Then the Lord threw the Egyptian army into confusion, making the wheels of their chariots come off so that they had difficulty driving. Then the water flowed back and covered the chariots and horsemen – the entire army of Pharaoh that had followed the Israelites into the sea. 'Not one of them survived' (Exodus 14:28). The high cost of Pharaoh's pride.

Consider some of the recent presidents whose mistakes changed the shape of their tenure. Had Richard Nixon admitted to his compliance in Watergate immediately, he might have been hailed as one of the greater presidents in history. Pride took over and he lost everything. Had Bill Clinton admitted to sexual indiscretions as soon as rumours emerged, he would have been forgiven. Some take the view that George W. Bush wanted to outdo his dad in Iraq and that America could have been spared incalculable consequences.

Rehoboam

Every year there are certain passages I dread having to read in my Bible reading plan – like Judges 19, 2 Samuel 11 and 1 Kings 12 when the proud and insecure Rehoboam rejected the wisdom of the elders at the beginning of his kingship. They urged him to lighten the harsh labour and yoke that his father King Solomon had put on them. Solomon had degenerated into a precarious spiritual state toward the end of his life and the nation was already in trouble. The elders' counsel was good. Succeeding Solomon need not have been such a hard act to follow. But Rehoboam was fatally unwise. He felt a need to prove himself – to demonstrate his manliness, authority, strength and wisdom. But it was all about his pride. He vowed to demonstrate that he was stronger than his father – '"My little finger is thicker than my father's waist"', a foolish comment to make (1 Kings 12:10). Rehoboam doubled the agony the people were already undergoing and the consequence for Israel was horrendous. A divided kingdom followed. Israel was never to be the same again. The high cost of Rehoboam's pride. He lost. Everyone lost.

The essence of Rehoboam's pride was the need to prove himself. Pride is the root of the need to prove ourselves. Why do we want to prove ourselves? Our ego is at stake. We need to be seen as wise and vindicated. Trying to prove ourselves always ends up in some kind of tragedy or embarrassment. As my old friend Pete Cantrell says, the greatest freedom is having nothing to prove. But when we do something to prove ourselves we step outside of the anointing of the Holy Spirit – every single time.

In my early years at Westminster Chapel I had a deep, deep need to prove myself. Being an American – and Kentuckian – plus following Dr Martyn Lloyd-Jones, gave me a dire need for assurance that I was worthy for the job. I will now relate a story which is probably the most painful memory during those twenty-five years there. Until now only Louise knows this story. One of my early converts at Westminster Chapel (the first person I baptised there) was a man by the name of Jay, a Jewish businessman from Los Angeles. He happened to be passing through London on his way to Moscow in 1977. His secretary in London persuaded him to come and hear me preach. He was converted instantly and we soon became great friends. He managed to get us Centre Court tickets at Wimbledon year after year. He introduced me to many famous people. In 1982 my book *Tithing* was published with a wonderful endorsement by Billy Graham. I was chuffed to have this endorsement. It meant more to me than it should have. I proudly sent the book to Jay, who (I found out later) was dying of cancer, thinking he would be impressed to see I had the attention of Billy Graham. But it badly backfired. Jay's wife (unconverted) and family took offence, thinking I was trying to get their money and get Jay to tithe. I was never welcome after that. I would give a thousand worlds if I had not sent that book to him, who died a few weeks later. Although the issue of tithing itself never crossed my mind, it was my silly pride nonetheless that was at the bottom of sending him the book in the first place. Had I not sent that book, I would have been warmly welcomed in that home and have further opportunity to witness for Christ. But my pride aborted that possibility forever. The high cost of my pride.

Uzziah

One of the longest reigning kings of Judah was Uzziah who reigned for fifty-two years. His accomplishments were amazing. 'As long as he sought the Lord, God gave him success' (2 Chronicles 26:5). He had many military successes. He rebuilt many towns, built towers in Jerusalem, had a well-trained army. His fame spread far and wide. He was greatly helped until he became powerful. But after that, '*his pride led to his downfall*' (2 Chronicles 26:15–16). One day he raged at the priests before the incense altar in the Lord's temple. 'Leprosy broke out on his forehead' and he had leprosy until the day he died. 'He lived in a separate house – leprous, and excluded from the temple of the Lord.' The words 'he had leprosy' overshadowed his monumental reign (2 Chronicles 26:19, 21). The high cost of pride.

Haman

Haman, a central character in the book of Esther, was not a part of the historic people of God, but his behaviour illustrates the high cost of pride. He had been honoured by King Xerxes and given a seat of honour higher than that of all other nobles. All royal officials knelt down to pay honour to Haman, for the king had commanded this concerning him. But Mordecai, the cousin of the Jewish Queen Esther, had for some reason refused to kneel down or pay Haman honour (Esther 3:1–2).

Mordecai's refusal to pay honour to Haman enraged Haman (Esther 3:5, 5:9). It was a blow to his pride. Haman was determined to get vengeance, not merely regarding Mordecai but managed to get King Xerxes to pass a law that would destroy all Jews (Esther 3:12–14), although no one but Mordecai knew that Esther herself was Jewish (Esther 2:10). But unbeknown to anybody up to now, Mordecai had shown his loyalty to Xerxes by exposing a plot that would have assassinated the king (Esther 6:2). When the king discovered it, he wanted to honour Mordecai for this deed. Without telling Haman who he had in mind, the king asked him what is a good way to honour someone? Thinking that the king must have meant Haman, Haman came up with a grandiose way for the king to carry this off (Esther 6:3–11). In the meantime Haman had prepared a gallows which was made for Mordecai (Esther 5:14). But moments before the hanging, Mordecai was exposed as being unscrupulous with the Queen whereupon the king ordered none other than Haman himself to be executed on the gallows he had prepared for Mordecai (Esther 7:6–10). The expression 'give a person enough rope and he will hang himself' comes from this account. Haman was hanged on the gallows made for Mordecai and the ultimate result was that the Jews were spared (Esther 8:3–11). It is a demonstration in any case of the high cost of pride – all this going back to Haman's being enraged because Mordecai would not honour him. 'Pride goes before destruction, a haughty spirit before a fall' (Proverbs 16:18).

Nebuchadnezzar and Belshazzar

We now examine the pride, fall but also restoration of another figure outside the people of God. Daniel's prophecy concerning King Nebuchadnezzar came true, all because the king had become arrogant. '"Is not this the great Babylon I have built as the royal residence, by my mighty power and for the glory of my majesty?"', said the king. A word then came to him, '"This is what is decreed for you, King Nebuchadnezzar: your royal authority has been taken from you. You will be driven away from people and will live with the wild animals; you will eat grass like cattle"'. This was immediately fulfilled. But this ordeal got his attention and he gave praise to the Most High God for the restoration of his sanity. The king's pride was then amazingly eclipsed by a true humility. Nebuchadnezzar concluded: 'those who walk in pride he is able to humble' (Daniel 4:28–37).

This passage is highly relevant for all of us. It shows how God notices the pride of kings and heads of state all over the world who think they can get away with arrogance.

King Belshazzar gave a banquet for his nobles, using the gold goblets that Nebuchadnezzar his father had taken from the temple in Jerusalem. Suddenly the fingers of a human hand appeared and wrote on the plaster of the wall. The king's face turned pale and he was so frightened that his knees knocked together and his legs gave way. The prophet Daniel was called to explain this extraordinary phenomenon. Daniel reminded Belshazzar of his father's pride, temporary insanity and restoration when he honoured the true God. '"But you his son, O Belshazzar, have not humbled yourself, *though you knew all this* ... you did not honour the God who holds in his hand your life and all your ways"' (Daniel 5:22–23 *emphasis* added). That very night Belshazzar was slain and the kingdom was given to Darius.

Herod Agrippa

Referred to as King Herod in Acts 12, Herod Agrippa had James the brother of John put to death by the sword and then proceeded to seize Peter also. Peter was miraculously delivered however (Acts 12:5–19). Later on Herod went to Caesarea. 'On the appointed day Herod, wearing his royal robes, sat on his throne and delivered a public address to the people. They shouted, "This is the voice of a god, not of a man."' Then, Luke writes, 'Immediately, because Herod did not give praise to God, an angel of the Lord struck him down, and he was eaten by worms and died' (Acts 12:21–23).

It is noteworthy that the reason for this sudden death was Herod's pride – his not giving glory to God. One might have thought Herod's punishment would be owing to his persecuting the apostles – and perhaps it was. But what precipitated God stepping in was Herod's pride.

I will say it again. These accounts of heads of state *outside* the covenant of God's own people show that God is in control of the whole world and takes notice of pride – wherever it is. This is a word that should encourage all of us when we see unbridled arrogance seemingly in control in a day when people have utterly forgotten God. But God is on the throne. 'The Lord detests all the proud of heart. Be sure of this: *They will not go unpunished*' (Proverbs 16:5). He will step in – never too late, never too early, but always just on time.

4

FORFEITING WISDOM

'The fear of the Lord is the beginning of wisdom, and knowledge
of the Holy One is understanding. When pride comes, then comes
disgrace, but with humility comes wisdom.'

Proverbs 9:10; 11:2

'Wisdom is the right use of knowledge. To know is not to be wise.
Many men know a great deal, and are all the greater fools for it.
There is no fool so great as a knowing fool. But to know how to use
knowledge is to have wisdom.'

C. H. Spurgeon (1834–1892)

Behind the high cost of pride is the absence of wisdom. When pride elbows its way into our lives, wisdom takes leave. The highest cost of pride is to forfeit wisdom.

Wisdom is the presence of *the mind of the Holy Spirit*. It is much, much more than presence of mind. Having mere 'presence of mind' is the ability to think and act calmly and efficiently, especially in an emergency. This might be given to an unbeliever through common grace, that 'special grace in nature' as we saw in Chapter 2. Having presence of mind certainly refers to a measure of wisdom.

But the highest form of wisdom is reserved for the true believer: the presence of the mind of the Spirit. The Holy Spirit always knows what to do *now*. The Holy Spirit always knows the next step forward. The Holy Spirit always has the key when the way forward eludes the greatest minds. Knowing exactly the right thing to do is a level of knowledge, then, that will escape the most brilliant mind unless the Holy Spirit unlocks the secret. The Spirit alone holds the secret as to *what to do next*. The Spirit knows exactly what to do next – whether in the next five weeks or the next five minutes. Wisdom is to know in advance what you will later wish you did. Only the Holy Spirit has this perfect foreknowledge. It is often said that we all have 20/20 hindsight vision. Wisdom is to have 20/20 foresight vision. To have this kind of knowledge is priceless. No brain, no intellect, no amount of earthly erudition possesses this secret. It is found in wisdom alone.

No wonder, then, that '"Wisdom is supreme; therefore get wisdom. Though it cost all you have, get understanding. Esteem her, and she will exalt you; embrace her, and she will honour you. She will set a garland of grace on your head and present you with a crown of splendour"' (Proverbs 4:7–8). 'I, wisdom, dwell together with prudence; I possess knowledge and discretion ... I love those who love me, and those who seek me find me. With me are riches and honour, enduring wealth and prosperity. My fruit is better than fine gold; what I yield surpasses choice silver' (Proverbs 8:12, 17–19).

Solomon

To ask for wisdom shows you are not too proud to do so. I have watched so many leaders, including heads of state, proceed with arrogance and a sense of sureness. But they so often lack wisdom. To quote Mrs Martyn Lloyd-Jones regarding a certain prime minister, 'Clever but not wise'. That is true with so many. If only they would accept the need for wisdom. It is humbling. It shows you don't know everything. It shows you need it. It is pride that will cause us to forfeit wisdom; it is humility that will lead to the awareness that we need it. Asking for wisdom is always the right thing to do. We may put wrong requests to God. I'm afraid I have done this many times, asking 'with wrong motives' (James 4:3). But you can be sure you are putting a right request to God when you ask for wisdom. After all, God answers our requests when we ask in

His will (1 John 5:14), so the one time you can be sure your request is in His will is in your appeal to Him for wisdom.

If you want to know how much God likes it when we ask for wisdom, just look at Solomon's wish. Solomon, son of David, was Israel's third king. God appeared to him in a dream and said (in so many words), 'Name it and claim it' (1 Kings 3:5)! How would you feel if God came to you and let you ask for anything you wanted? What would you ask for? Have you thought about this? Solomon could not have made God happier. Solomon asked for wisdom. God was *so* pleased with this request that he said to Solomon, '"Since you have asked for this and not for long life or wealth for yourself, nor have asked for the death of your enemies but for discernment in administering justice, I will do what you have asked … Moreover, I will give you what you have not asked for – both riches and honour – so that in your lifetime you will have no equal among kings"' (1 Kings 3:11–13).

The early church's real need

James urged early Christian Jews to ask for wisdom. 'If any of you lacks wisdom, he should ask God, who gives generously to all without finding fault, and it will be given to him' (James 1:5). Although writing in Greek to Hellenistic Jews scattered everywhere, James' burden arose out of the situation of the early church in Jerusalem. James knew they needed wisdom. They were discouraged. They were not growing. There was a time when it seemed that the Christian faith would take off – it was certainly the wave of the future. They had a wonderful beginning, and had encouragement from the miracle of the forty-year-old man who had never walked. Many were converted (Acts 3:6–10, 4:4). But after a few years all this seemed to change. They had dwindling numbers. They were no doubt looking for some kind of breakthrough.

James suggests that their need was for wisdom. What James means by wisdom somewhat sounds like what Paul means by *agape* love. James speaks of 'the humility that comes from wisdom' (James 3:13). It 'is first of all pure; then peace-loving, considerate, submissive, full of mercy and good fruit, impartial and sincere (James 3:17; cf. 1 Corinthians 13:4–6). As some readers may know, I was brought up in the Church of the Nazarene. The founder was Phineas Bresee (1838–1915). In his last days he had one message for early Nazarenes: 'Keep the glory down.' What did he mean by that? By 'glory' he meant the immediate presence of God. There was a touch of God on early Nazarenes that explained their rapid growth. People would come to their services to laugh or scoff. They got converted instead. It was this 'glory' that did it. Early Nazarenes did not have great intellects nor were they wealthy people. But they had the 'glory'. Bresee knew that if they ever lost that, they were *finished*.

This is much the same thing as the wisdom that comes from above which James had in mind. The Greek word is *sophia*. In ancient Hellenistic literature it denoted a quality, not an activity. *Sophia* implied unusual knowledge and ability. It was thought to be the possession of the gods alone. But I have defined this wisdom as the presence of the mind of the Spirit. It is what God wants to give us. This is what the early church needed more than anything else.

There were other words James might have chosen which, for all I know, would have pleased certain Jews more. He might have referred to *philosophia* – which referred to rhetoric and ability to dispute. Some might have assumed this was the need of the day. James might have used the word *techna* – a reference to art, skill or craft. Some might have thought the early church needed more talented people. James might have used the word *phren* – a reference to cleverness or intellect. Some might have thought the early church needed stronger intellects. We do know they were having some problems of identity in that they seemed preoccupied with the kind of people who were showing up when they met. Sadly they showed partiality to rich people, those who came to their assemblies with the 'gold ring and fine clothes' (James 2:2). Prosperity was very important to Jews – then and now – and they may have thought that having the rich and famous would cause more people to show up for church. Wrong, says James, you need to ask for wisdom. Normally it was Greeks who sought after wisdom, Jews required a sign (see 1 Corinthians 1:22). But James takes them back to their ancient Hebrew heritage – to the rich wisdom literature which was such a big part of their background.

But the Bible says that true wisdom begins not with intellect, education, fame, wealth or talent but with the *fear of the Lord* (see Proverbs 1:7; 9:10). 'Blessed is the man who finds wisdom, the man who gains understanding' (Proverbs 3:13). 'Get wisdom, get understanding' (Proverbs 4:5). '... wisdom is more precious than rubies, and nothing you desire can compare with her' (Proverbs 8:11). And listen to this: 'The fear of the Lord *teaches a man wisdom, and humility comes before honour*' (Proverbs 15:33).

The great deterrent to wisdom is *pride.* Isn't this amazing? The most important thing in the world – wisdom – is closer than our feet, closer than the air we breathe! We can't buy it, you can't negotiate for it, you can't manipulate yourself into getting it, your best friend can't give it to you, political favours won't make it come, being famous doesn't bring you one step closer. It begins with the fear of the Lord; indeed, the fear of the Lord teaches wisdom. The thing is, when wisdom emerges, you are a fool if you take credit for it! Only God can grant His hidden knowledge; it by-passes the brain.

But we are too proud to want wisdom that much. The fear of the Lord is costly. It demands a change in our lifestyle. So we will seek for solutions *anywhere* but the fear of the Lord!

On one occasion when Jesus was doing miracles, the people asked a very interesting question: '"Where did this man get these things?" ... "What's this wisdom that has been given him, that he even does miracles!"' (Mark 6:2). You might have expected them to ask, 'Where did he get this power?' But they asked, 'Where did he get this wisdom?' Could it be that wisdom is the mother of the power we long to see displayed?

Stephen

One of the greatest men in the early church was Stephen. He was among the original seven deacons (Acts 6:5). To be a deacon, one had to be 'full of the Spirit and wisdom' (Acts 6:3). This shows you can be Spirit-filled and still not have wisdom! Indeed, I'm afraid I have known not a few people who were Spirit-filled but lacked wisdom. Wisdom is not listed among the fruits of the Spirit (Galatians 5:22–23) but it leads the list of gifts in 1 Corinthians 12:8–10. Strangely it seems to be the last thing so many are interested in! But it is one of the great needs of the hour.

Stephen had this wisdom. When unbelieving Jews began to argue with him, 'they could not stand up against the wisdom the Spirit gave him as he spoke' (Acts 6:10). It is the level of anointing I want more than anything in the world. If God came to me as he did Solomon, I think this is exactly what I would ask for. Jesus did promise this if we stood before kings. '... do not worry about what to say or how to say it. At that time you will be given what to say, for it will not be you speaking, but the Spirit of your Father speaking through you' (Matthew 10:19–20).

I have known two occasions in my life when I depended on Matthew 10:20 – '... it will not be you speaking, but the Spirit of your Father speaking through you'. The first was in Carlisle, Ohio when I was on the carpet before the authorities in a denomination for my teaching. That morning I was given Matthew 10:20 quite miraculously. It held me when I stood before certain hierarchical ministers for my doctrine. The other occasion was when I was invited to meet the late Yasser Arafat. I felt helpless but was given words in Ramallah that resulted in my having a surprising friendship with him. I won't know until I get to heaven how much good was accomplished, but I am certain that Matthew 10:20 was in operation on the five occasions I spent time with him.

The thing about wisdom that must be grasped is that it is not natural. It has nothing to do with one's education or IQ. It comes to one thing: the fear of the Lord. This means that, although it is costly, it is nonetheless free of charge. Yes, there is a price to pay: swallowing our pride and admitting to our true need. 'Trust in the Lord with all your heart and lean not on your own understanding; in all your ways acknowledge him, and he will make your paths straight' (Proverbs 3:5–6).

Two kinds of wisdom

James says there is wisdom that comes from *above* and 'wisdom' which is *earthly*. Earthly wisdom is characterised by bitter envy and selfish ambition. It is 'unspiritual, demonic'. This wisdom comes as a consequence of our pride (James 3:14–16). You find this in surprising places – in church, government, universities and in those who live to impress you by their great brains and clever gimmicks. It is when one is like Nebuchadnezzar who boasts of what 'I have done'. You see it in lawyers, physicians, professors, presidents, senators, members of parliament, preachers, bishops, archbishops and popes.

The wisdom that comes from above however, is like the wisdom of Jesus – (James 3:17–18) 'pure, ... easy to be entreated, full of mercy ...' (KJV) '... submissive ... Peacemakers who sow in peace raise a harvest of righteousness' (NIV). This wisdom is what we forfeit when the opinions of people mean more than God's favour. The result may be theological wisdom, when one is kept from serious error (John 7:17). It could mean wisdom for guidance (Proverbs 3:6), or wisdom regarding your calling and gifting (Ephesians 5:17).

The secret of the Lord

This wisdom is a secret. That means you can't find it unless the One who knows where it is gives it to you. This point cannot be overemphasised. You can look for it, go on a forty-day fast, read the best of books, see a psychiatrist or psychologist, get a university degree, mix with the most intellectual people and spend time on the Internet. *You will not find it* unless the One who has it gives it to you. According to James, He loves to give it. He gives generously to all without finding fault but we must ask in faith (James 1:5–6). Since God alone can give faith (you can't work it up), you have to go to Him on bended knee. Yes, to the One who said He will have mercy on whom He will have mercy (Romans 9:15).

Wisdom, then, is a sovereign gift. 'The secret of the Lord is with them that fear him' (Psalms 25:14 KJV), he 'confides in those who fear him' (NIV). He will withhold it from a man with a Ph.D. and give it to the lowliest person on the planet if that person fears the Lord. Nothing pleases God more than giving this wisdom. The requirement: swallow your pride.

Sexual indiscretion and pride

Pride is not the only thing that causes one to forfeit wisdom. Sexual impurity is proof that one has parted from wisdom. If we are indiscrete in the area of sexual purity, the secret of the Lord will elude us, no matter how mature, famous, intelligent or educated we are otherwise. Indeed, over and over again comes the warning in Proverbs about the adulterous woman, the foreign or strange woman (e.g. Proverbs 2:16; 5:2–20; 6:20–7:27; 9:13–18).

It could be argued too that pride is often at the bottom of sexual promiscuity, as when one seeks affirmation from the opposite sex. Sexual sin is often rooted in the need to prove oneself. The need to be admired often begins with flirting. The imprudent remark may be a spark that sets a forest on fire (James 3:5ff). When James states that the wisdom which is from above is 'first of all pure' (James 3:17) he implies that sexual purity among other things is inherent in heavenly wisdom.

Extreme caution

You could be proud of your wisdom. This is a huge danger. This is why we have this warning, 'Be not wise in your own conceits' (Romans 12:16 KJV). 'Do not be wise in your own eyes' (Proverbs 3:7). This is a subtle but very real temptation. The moment you sense you have a touch of wisdom – like humility – it disappears instantly. Be aware of this. Charles Spurgeon once said, 'I looked to Christ and the Dove flew in I looked to the Dove and he disappeared'. Keep your eyes on God with fear and trembling lest you become proud. Being proud of your humility however is actually an impossibility because once you think you are humble, you have lost it. So with wisdom: be extremely aware that you can become a target of the devil if you have had occasion to be wise in a situation.

Wisdom as a gift could reside in some people. By that I mean some may have wisdom almost continually. People like this (and they are few) must be most guarded. But if pride slips in, they too will look like utter fools at the end of the day. Solomon did. A person's strength is often their downfall.

But if we will covet the presence of the mind of the Spirit – which means being on good terms with the Holy Spirit by never grieving him (see Ephesians 4:30), it will keep us on the straight and narrow. Just maybe we will be preserved from the pride that destroys wisdom.

What a thing to forfeit – this precious commodity. More valuable than gold and diamonds. Its price is incalculable. God alone has it. He has the secret. He loves to give it. But only to those who will show contempt for their pride.

5

MODESTY

'For who makes you different from anyone else? What do you have that you did not receive? And if you did receive it, why do you boast as though you did not?'
    I Corinthians 4:7

'Mr. Attlee is a very modest man. But then he has much to be modest about.'
    Winston Churchill (1874–1965)

'Modesty is my best quality.'
    Jack Benny (1894–1974)

I might have called this chapter 'the inexcusableness of pride' because nobody has a good excuse for being proud. But we all manage to get proud nonetheless! There is something in the fallen human heart that causes us to pretend. The truth is, we are all like Clement Attlee who, said Churchill, had much to be modest about. So too with the great Sir Winston Churchill! But although, like most Americans, I admire him greatly, based on what I know about him, I would not have wanted the task of convincing Sir Winston that he had much to be modest about.

The word modesty means being humble or self-effacing. It is perhaps best understood in terms of what it is not: the opposite of pride, arrogance, vanity. It is having a moderate estimate of one's own merits; not being boastful. Possibly the best synonym is unpretentiousness. I reckon the best single word to describe Jesus is his unpretentiousness.

The truth is, we all have much to be modest about. This is why Paul asked some arrogant Corinthians, 'What do you have that you did not receive? And if you did receive it, why do you boast as though you did not?' (1 Corinthians 4:7). The further truth is, we are all *nothing* in ourselves. We are what we are by the sheer grace of God. This is the point Paul tried to make with the Romans: '... there is a remnant chosen by grace. And if by grace, then it is no longer by works; if it were, grace would no longer be grace' (Romans 11:5–6). The point of being chosen by grace is that we have no grounds for boasting. We have been chosen and saved 'not because of anything we have done but because of his own purpose and grace' (2 Timothy 1:9). 'For it is by grace you have been saved, through faith – and this not from yourselves, it is the gift of God – not by works, so that no one can boast' (Ephesians 2:8–9).

Lumps of clay

Whether it be creation or salvation – common grace or saving grace – we have no basis for boasting. We are lumps of clay, says Paul. No matter what we turn out to be, we are in the end lumps of clay that God moulded as he chose to do. ' "Shall what is formed say to him who formed it, 'Why did you make me like this?' " Does not the potter have the right to make out of the same lump of clay some pottery for noble purposes and some for common use?' (Romans 9:20–21). If one turns out to be an Einstein or a Rachmaninoff, a Moses or a Paul, there is one – only one – explanation: the sovereign grace of God.

But we are loath to see this! This is painful. It hurts to realise that we are totally dependent upon God for all we are.

'But', says someone, 'God gave us free will and we are his workmanship and made to do good works, as in Ephesians 2:10'. Yes. But who can boast that what he or she turns out to be was accomplished apart from (1) the way we were born or (2) the Holy Spirit's help?

There are at least three predictable reactions to this truth. One is to scream in anger at God – and to defy Him by trying all the harder to achieve something in your own strength. This seems most foolish. Another reaction is to deny the very existence of God and assume an utterly humanistic perspective – to prove how good you are. The third is to accept humbly the truth that you and I are nothing except by the very grace of God – and then bend the knee and worship.

King David and the Temple

At the height of his kingship, David hoped to build the temple of God in Jerusalem. It is the one big thing in David's life that he was not able to achieve, although he aspired to be the one to build the temple. God said to him through Nathan the prophet in so many words, 'No, David, you cannot do it'. This must have been a severe blow to David. Nathan was instructed by God to say to David, 'I took you from the pasture and from following the flock to be ruler over my people Israel'. God proceeded to remind David not only of his humble beginnings but of the other things God had done for David – sparing his life after twenty years of running from Saul, being made king over Judah, then king over Israel, then conquering Jerusalem, then bringing the ark into Jerusalem, not to mention that God cut off *all* of David's enemies (see 2 Samuel 7:1–11). God could have added: 'The Messiah will come through your loins, and what about those Psalms you wrote as a legacy? So David, I've been pretty good to you, have I not?'

What do you suppose was the response of the only person in the Bible called 'a man after God's own heart' (1 Samuel 13:14)? Here was David's exact response: '"Who am I, O Sovereign Lord, and what is my family, that you have brought me this far? And as if this were not enough in your sight, O Sovereign Lord, you have also spoken about the future of the house of your servant. Is this your usual way of dealing with man, O Sovereign Lord?"' (2 Samuel 7:18–19). David never forgot that he was chosen and taken from the 'sheep pens' (Psalms 78:71). He knew he was *nothing*.

During the time that John Newton (1725–1807) was the vicar of Olney, Buckinghamshire, he had a practice of writing a new hymn every week. These hymns can be found in the Olney Hymnal along with many of William Cowper's (1731–1800). Newton wrote the new hymn based upon the text of his sermon. On one of those Sundays he had decided to preach on the account of David being told by Nathan the prophet that he could not build the temple of God in Jerusalem. When Newton read those words, 'Who am I, O Lord God? and what is my house, that thou hast brought me hitherto?' (2 Samuel 7:18 KJV), he reflected on his own life. Newton had been a profligate man which included being right in the middle of bringing slaves from Africa to England. But he was gloriously converted. 2 Samuel 7:18 is what inspired 'Amazing grace, how sweet the sound'. When you get to verse three the words of 2 Samuel 7:18 can be traced via the words,

'Through many dangers, toils and snares I have already come,
Tis grace that brought me *safe thus far* and grace will lead me home'.

John Newton *knew* he had nothing of which to boast. Following David, he never forgot his upbringing and maintained a life of gratitude. When we lived in Oxford we used to take friends from America to Olney just to see what Newton had written to be put on his tombstone:

JOHN NEWTON
Clerk.
Once an infidel and libertine.
a servant of slaves in Africa.
Was.
by the rich mercy
of our Lord and Saviour
JESUS CHRIST.
Preserved. restored. pardoned.
and appointed to preach the faith
he had long laboured to destroy.

David stated, 'The boundary lines have fallen for me in pleasant places; surely I have a delightful inheritance' (Psalms 16:6). This eliminated all basis for boasting. We may not all be King Davids, we may not all be famous hymn writers and not all attain to a high profile, but none of us has a right to be proud. We are what we are by the grace of God. 'What do you have that you did not receive? And if you did receive it, why do you boast as though you did not?' (1 Corinthians 4:7). Perhaps this reminder would have brought the Corinthians down a notch or two. Does this verse do that to you?

How dare we boast about anything in us, whether it be some apparent virtue or achievement, when in fact it is what God gave us. If you and I would take a moment – and pause. Reflect. We surely know we are nothing in ourselves. Is this not true? Humbling, isn't it?

Jesus' vindication

When God became man in the person of Jesus Christ 'he made himself nothing' (Philippians 2:5). The relevant Greek word is *ekenosen* – 'emptied'. The Second Person of the Godhead emptied himself of all that was rightfully His and became nothing. The Greek word means to be deprived of content or possession. The King James Version says that He made Himself of 'no reputation' – which of course was true. But the literal translation means that the God-man emptied Himself of glory – the glory He had with the Father before the world began (John 17:5). Because Jesus voluntarily emptied Himself, He in fact had a right not to be modest! But He was. He chose to be modest. He did not stroll around Galilee or Jerusalem saying, 'If you only knew what I gave up', 'Don't you realise how wonderful I am?', 'Do you think you appreciate me as you should?' or 'I deserve your worship and adoration'.

Jesus not only chose to empty Himself but never told anybody He had done this. Such an observation came from the apostles by the Holy Spirit after Jesus ascended to heaven. During the time of His sojourn before His resurrection, it never crossed anybody's mind that He was God in the flesh. This revelation came by the

Holy Spirit. Years later the Apostle John could reflect upon the inestimable privilege that was his to be with the person of Jesus: 'We have seen his glory, glory as of the only Son from the Father, full of grace and truth' (John 1:14 ESV)

Jesus was vindicated by the Holy Spirit (1 Timothy 3:16). This means (1) that the Holy Spirit witnessed to Him that the Father was pleased with Him. That totally satisfied Him; He needed no more approval. And yet it was an internal vindication. Had it been an external vindication, everybody would have seen with their own eyes how glorious Jesus was – that He was God in the flesh. The external vindication would come later – much later, when every knee shall bow and every tongue confess that Jesus Christ is Lord to the glory of God the Father (Philippians 2:10–11).

Neither did Jesus have a need to get anybody's approval. Can you imagine Jesus saying to the disciples after the Sermon on the Mount, 'How did I do? Was that not a pretty good sermon, Peter?' Jesus got his approval from the Father. Not only that; after Jesus was raised from the dead, He did not show up at Pilate's house and say, '*Surprise!*'. His internal vindication continued after His resurrection.

This internal vindication also means that (2) you and I see His glory only by the Holy Spirit. How do we convince another person of what we believe? Can we take them to see Jesus with their natural eyes? No. In other words, not only did Jesus Himself get his vindication by the witness of the Holy Spirit, but so do we – by what the Spirit reveals to us about Him. We are not able to convince another person of the truth of Jesus unless they too have the internal testimony of the Holy Spirit. You and I have not seen Jesus with our natural eyes at the right hand of God. 'Though you have not seen him, you love him; and even though you do not see him now, you believe in him and are filled with an expressible and glorious joy' (1 Peter 1:8).

While Jesus was on earth, then, He was the epitome of modesty. And yet He had nothing to be modest about! He is the only person who ever lived who had the right to be admired and adulated, but His deity was hidden.

'Veiled in flesh the Godhead see!
Hail the incarnate Deity!
Pleased as Man with men to dwell,
Jesus, our Immanuel.'

Charles Wesley (1707–88)

His choice to be 'nothing' was maintained throughout His days on earth by being unpretentious. This was a part of His glory. He never put on 'airs'. He made no attempt to impress anybody. He was approachable. 'Sinners' felt at home with Him' (Luke 15:2). He was so humble that He was almost completely unnoticed. Who would notice a 'root out of dry ground'? Indeed, 'he had no beauty or majesty to attract us to him, nothing in his appearance that we should desire him' (Isaiah 53:2–3). Although Jesus had the Spirit without any limit (John 3:34), He was almost certainly devoid of the 'charisma' that often characterises successful politicians or movie stars. In fact Judas had to notify those who were sent to arrest Him by kissing Him (Matthew 26:48). He merely blended in with the rest.

You and I are called to follow in His steps. 'When they hurled their insults at him, he did not retaliate; when he suffered, he made no threats. Instead he entrusted himself to him who judges justly' (1 Peter 2:21–23). This means we are called to modesty. You and I should make every attempt to be modest. That means we will do nothing to attract attention to ourselves. We will say nothing that makes us look good or would be self-vindicating. He should always let the other person praise us, making sure we are not eliciting praise. We should make every effort to get the praise that comes from God only and eschew fishing for compliments from people.

Are we approachable? The leper knew in his heart he could approach Jesus (Matthew 8:1ff). The common people heard Jesus gladly (Mark 12:37 KJV). The wisdom that comes from above is 'full of mercy' (James 3:17). In a word: graciousness.

Perhaps only the direct and immediate presence of God would expose our vanity. When Isaiah saw the glory of the Lord he said, 'Woe is me!' (Isaiah 6:5). Our immodesty therefore betrays not merely our lack of humility and how full of ourselves we are, but how distant we are from the presence of God. May God grant such an outpouring of his Holy Spirit on us that we will see our conceit and boastfulness and bring us to our knees with a desire evermore to be like Jesus.

6

WHEN THE ANOINTING LIFTS

'I saw the Spirit come down from heaven as a dove and remain on him.'
    John 1:32

'And do not grieve the Holy Spirit of God, with whom you were sealed for the day of redemption. Get rid of all bitterness, rage and anger . . . along with every form of malice. Be kind and compassionate to one another, forgiving each other, just as in Christ God forgave you.'
    Ephesians 4:30–32

'To test a modest man's modesty do not investigate if he ignores applause, find out if he abides criticism.'
    Frank Grillparzer (1791–1872)

This chapter actually extends the theme 'the inexcusableness of pride'. We saw that any virtue or achievement we have is traced to the utter grace of God. We are therefore foolish to gloat or to take credit for any good thing in us. But if there is any doubt as to our having no right to be proud about ourselves, this becomes clear when we see what we are like when the anointing of the Holy Spirit lifts from us.

The anointing – the power of the Holy Spirit – is a tricky term. In the Old Testament it could refer to the kingship (1 Samuel 24:6).

The anointing is in every Christian (1 John 2:20), and yet we know that the Holy Spirit can be grieved. The word translated 'grieved' in Ephesians 4:30 comes from a Greek word that means to have your feelings hurt. We can hurt the Holy Spirit's feelings. The Holy Spirit, the Third Person of the Godhead, is a very, very sensitive person. When I wrote *Sensitivity of the Holy Spirit*, I wanted to call the book the 'Hyper-sensitivity of the Spirit', but my publisher (rightly) talked me out of it. But that is the point – the Holy Spirit is hyper-sensitive; His feelings are hurt *so* easily. When we refer to a person as being hyper-sensitive it is certainly not a compliment. But that is exactly the way the Holy Spirit is! You may want to say (I'm afraid I have), 'He ought not be like that'. The only reply: but He is the only Holy Spirit you've got, so get over it – and get used to His ways!

God lamented of ancient Israel because 'they have not known my ways' (Hebrews 3:10). Basically we need to learn two things from God: (1) His word (the Bible) and (2) His ways (His manner of dealing with people). You get to know His word by taking the time to read the Bible. By the way, do you have a Bible reading plan? You need one. I can say that I have read the Bible through nearly 40 times – and the New Testament many, many more times. It is because I use a plan that tells me precisely where to read every day. None of us is so spiritual that he or she can just feel 'led' from day to day to open the Bible and start reading. You need the discipline that will keep you in the word – daily. You will never be sorry you did this.

You get to know God's 'ways' by how much you spend time with Him and how you discern the anointing coming down and lifting. Children spell love T–I–M–E. What if God spells love like that? How much do you pray? You get to know a person by how much time you give them. I always urged every member of Westminster Chapel to spend no less than 30 minutes a day in quiet time. I urge ministers to spend at least one hour a day. Martin Luther prayed two hours a day. John Wesley was up every morning at 4 a.m. to pray two hours before he proceeded into the day. But where are the Luthers today? Where are the Wesleys? According to a poll, the typical church leader in Britain and America (I wish it weren't true) spends an average of four minutes a day in quiet time. (And you wonder why the church is powerless?) In any case, you get to know God's ways by spending time with Him *and* being able to sense His presence and His absence and exactly when the Dove may have lifted. I would define spirituality as closing the 'time gap' between sin and repentance. In other words, how long does it take you to admit you were *wrong*? For some it takes years. For some it takes months. For some it is weeks. Perhaps for some it is days. For some hours, for some minutes and – just maybe – for some it only takes a few seconds to notice that you have grieved the Holy Spirit. When you narrow the time gap to seconds you are getting closer to knowing God's 'ways'.

This may be one of the reasons the Spirit is depicted in the New Testament as a dove. The dove is a shy, sensitive bird. Pigeons and doves are in the same family, but they are quite different in their make-up or 'personalities'. You can train a pigeon, but you can't train a dove. Pigeons can be domesticated, the dove is basically a wild bird. Pigeons are boisterous, doves are gentle; pigeons are belligerent, doves are peaceful.

John the Baptist knew that Jesus was the true Messiah because the dove came down and 'remained' on Jesus. I wish he remained on me! I know what it is (I wish it happened more often) for the Holy Spirit to come down on me. The feeling is sheer bliss – the peace, the joy, the feeling that God is in total control of everything. One wants to say, 'Please stay, please don't leave'. But as the day progresses, one finds the dove lifted – he flew away. This of course is speaking metaphorically. The truth is, the Holy Spirit never leaves us (John 14:16); indeed, we are 'sealed for the day of redemption' (Ephesians 4:30). But it is nonetheless true that the anointing can 'lift', as it were; that is, as if the dove flew off and left us to ourselves. The dove came on Jesus and *remained*. This tells you a lot about Jesus. The dove was 'at home' with Jesus. Jesus never – *ever* – grieved the Holy Spirit.

51

Left to ourselves

When the dove, or anointing lifts, a number of things can happen. We can lose a sense of God's presence. We find it virtually impossible to understand Scripture. We can be irritable. We forfeit the liberty of the Spirit. Our gift may not even function very easily. It is as though the lifting of the anointing means we are *left to ourselves*.

Hezekiah

When we are left to ourselves we discover exactly what we are like! Take King Hezekiah, for example. Consider this description of him:

'He did what was right in the eyes of the Lord, just as his father David had done. He removed the high places, smashed the sacred stones and cut down the Asherah poles. He broke into pieces the bronze snake Moses had made, for up to that time the Israelites had been burning incense to it ... Hezekiah trusted in the Lord, the God of Israel. There was no one like him among all the kings of Judah, either before him or after him. He held fast to the Lord and did not cease to follow him; he kept the commands the Lord had given Moses. And the Lord was with him; he was successful in whatever he undertook' (2 Kings 18:3–7).

Hezekiah had a remarkable career indeed. During his kingship he purified the temple (2 Chronicles 29), the fearful threat of Sennacherib was miraculously stopped (2 Kings 19:35ff), God added fifteen years to Hezekiah's life when he was supposed to die (2 Kings 20:6), Israel and Judah enjoyed the greatest celebration of Passover – ever (2 Chronicles 30) and he made the pool and tunnel that brought water into the city of Jerusalem (2 Kings 20:20).

When you read the description of Hezekiah and observe his achievements, you think 'Wow! What a mighty man of God!' Perhaps you have had this similar impression of other great men of God you have known – or known about. When you hear them preach – or observe them from afar – you have put them way up high on a pedestal. Have you ever wondered what *your own* hero would be like if God were to leave him or her to themselves? It may not be a pretty sight.

Let's look again Hezekiah. There is more about him that we may not want to know. It is said of King Hezekiah that 'God left him to test him and to know everything that was in his heart' (2 Chronicles 32:31). This perfectly describes what I mean by being left to ourselves and is therefore what lay behind Hezekiah's disappointing behaviour at the end of his life. This is when Hezekiah's heart became 'proud' and did not respond to the kindness shown him (2 Chronicles 32:25). Pride and ingratitude often go together. I have known some people who never like to say 'thank you'– or, at least, are uncomfortable showing thankfulness. God had been exceedingly good to Hezekiah but he became too proud to show appreciation. 'Therefore the Lord's wrath was on him and on Judah and Jerusalem' (2 Chronicles 32:25). And keep in mind also that the last thing said of Hezekiah was that he thought, 'There will be security in my lifetime', virtually ignoring that his own folly would be punished in the following generation (Isaiah 39:1–8). This is the same Hezekiah that had been extolled earlier!

I am told that statistics show nowadays one out of three church leaders end well. I am 75. My life isn't over – yet. I hope to end well. But as Yogi Berra, the great New York Yankee baseball catcher, used to say, 'It ain't over 'til it's over'.

By the way, never – ever – take for granted this matter of remembering to show thanks. I was given a wake-up call regarding this. I will never forget it (I talk about it in my book *Just Say Thanks*). All I can say here is that I made a commitment in 1986 to become a grateful man – and to show this partly by thanking God *every single day* for everything I can think of over the previous 24 hours.

Here is why. I have learned that God loves gratitude, God hates ingratitude, and gratitude must be taught. Those three principles need to be absorbed by all of us. We are made in the image of God. God loves to be thanked. So do we. A person may say, 'Thank you' to us for something we did for them and we say, 'Don't mention it'. But woe to that person who doesn't mention it! We all hate ingratitude. So does God. When ten lepers were healed, only one came back to say, 'Thank you', to Jesus. His immediate response: 'Where are the other nine?' (Luke 17:17). Paul describes a people who knew that God existed but they neither glorified him 'nor gave thanks to him' (Romans 1:21). Paul also describes the condition of people in the last days, including that they would be 'ungrateful' (2 Timothy 3:2).

Job

Listen to this description of Job: 'blameless and upright; he feared God and shunned evil' (Job 1:1). When he began to be tested quite severely, 'Job did not sin by charging God with wrongdoing' (Job 1:22). When the testing increased and he was in considerable stress and pain, his wife said to him, 'Are you still holding to your integrity? Curse God and die!' His reply to her: 'You are talking like a foolish woman' so that in all he went through 'Job did not sin in what he said' (Job 2:9–10). So far, so good: Job looks like a true hero – a saint of the ages.

But there is more. His 'friends' came along and began to wear him down. Little by little one sees the crack in Job's armour. He begins to get defensive. He starts retorting as his 'friends' continued to question his integrity. In the end he became self-righteous to the core – like all of us (Job 32:1). Oh dear. What happened? The anointing on Job lifted along the way and Job then revealed what he was potentially like all along. But no one would have thought it! It was not until Job was left to himself that we were given to see what was in his heart.

By the way, do you think you are any different? Do you believe you are a cut above other people who have their clay feet? Was not Solomon right when he said, '– for there is no one who does not sin' (1 Kings 8:46)?

But the anointing returned to Job. After God answered Job out of the whirlwind, or storm, he said to God, '"I am unworthy – how can I reply to you? I put my hand over my mouth. I spoke once, but I have no answer – twice, but I will say no more"' (Job 40:4–5). Yes, when the anointing returns we have the sense to put our hands on our mouths! He ended up saying, '"My ears had heard of you but now my eyes have seen you. Therefore I despise myself and repent in dust and ashes"' (Job 42:6).

How gracious God was with Job – and with you and me.

In a word: when the anointing lifts from us and leaves us to ourselves we not only forget to be thankful but become self-righteous. We take God for granted. If we aren't careful we will even begin to think that he owes us something – a very bad condition to fall into. God owes us nothing. But when we are left to ourselves we often begin to feel sorry for ourselves and imagine vain things about God. It can be traced to being proud.

There is more. When we are left to ourselves bitterness almost always surfaces. Indeed, the chief way we grieve the Holy Spirit is by bitterness – that inward anger and rage inside. It may come from being mistreated, hurt or misunderstood. Whatever the reason, bitterness grieves the Holy Spirit – resulting in a lifting of the anointing. I'm sorry, but the Holy Spirit won't bend the rules for any of us. We may think that since we are 'veterans' in the kingdom of God – having been converted for a good while, God gives us special indemnity. Wrong. He won't bend the rules for you or me, no matter how long we have been Christians, how valuable our gifts or how well known we might be.

Totally forgiving others

To put it another way, when the Dove comes down on me I find it easy to forgive. Some readers may know about my book *Total Forgiveness*. When you have totally forgiven the person who has been hurtful or unfair, you won't gossip to anybody 'what they did' or who it was. You will not throw up their past, you will not say anything to cause fear in them, you will not let them feel guilty, you will let them save face (as opposed to 'rubbing their noses in it'), you will protect them from their dark secrets, you will bless them – which means praying for them to be blessed, and you *keep doing it*. On this last point once is not enough! Total forgiveness is a 'life sentence'. Like a pill you may have to take as long as you live, so too with forgiving others; you must do it today, tomorrow, next week, next year. Otherwise the devil will remind you of 'what they did' and get you all churned up. When the Holy Spirit comes powerfully alongside, it isn't so hard to do all I have outlined above.

When the Holy Spirit makes it easy, then, how can you take credit for it? How can you feel proud that 'you' did something? To the spiritual person the supernatural seems natural. As the manna in the desert seemed natural after it lasted so long, so too when you walk in the Spirit and see amazing things take place, the temptation might be to think it was *you* – when in fact it was God at work and not you. Once you begin to think you have 'arrived', you also risk grieving the Spirit – which means the lifting of the anointing.

Therefore the moment the anointing lifts, and the flesh sets in, you find yourself holding a grudge. You want to hurt the person's reputation, you want them to be in fear, you make them feel guilty, you throw up what they did – and try to make them feel awful, you might even gossip what you know. Moreover, you find it almost impossible to pray that God will bless them. When you are left to yourself you want God to punish them; when the Dove returns you ask God to bless them. After all, total forgiveness is not natural; it is supernatural. When the Dove comes down you start doing that which defies a natural explanation, but when the anointing lifts you do what is natural and what seems right to you. Remember too that there is a way that seems right but the end being the ways of death (see Proverbs 14:12).

Here is the point. What *seems* right to us when the Dove has lifted will almost always be wrong. This is because when we are left to ourselves what 'seems' right is being governed by the flesh not the Spirit. But once the Dove lifts and you are walking according to the flesh, you will probably start pointing the finger, finding fault, reminding one of their past sins – sending them on a most painful guilt trip.

One thing is dead certain: you realise exactly what you are like when you are left to yourself. Any prideful feelings you may have had turn into an embarrassing reality. You find yourself thinking, 'I can't believe I said that.' 'I can't believe I did that.' 'I thought I was beyond behaving like that.' It is like the spark that causes the forest fire (James 3:5). 'Earthly' wisdom takes charge: bitter envy, selfish ambition, disorder and every evil practice (James 3:14ff).

The bottom line is this: when we are left to ourselves, it is pretty hard to feel we have overcome pride! For pride is what feeds the carnal nature. As we have seen above, anger is what causes us to lose our temper; pride is what keeps us angry.

Perhaps the severest test to our humility is how we handle criticism. When the flesh takes over you will start being critical. The question is, can *you* take criticism? Meekness is the virtue of taking criticism without retorting. It is turning the other cheek (Matthew 5:39). You might hastily assume that a person is meek or modest because they ignore applause. The test is how they handle criticism! If you can take criticism as readily as you can cope with praise, you show remarkable maturity. But this maturity too is by the grace of the Holy Spirit so that you cannot feel proud! You are a fool if you do.

All hell can break loose by one spark – the unguarded comment that starts a forest fire. That fire can last for hours or days. Whatever the result, you should at least learn this one thing from such an unhappy episode: you have to admit that pride was at the bottom of it all.

There is a lovely story I tell in *Sensitivity of the Spirit* that will bear repeating in this book. A British couple were sent by their denomination to Israel as missionaries a few years ago. They were given a home in which to live near Jerusalem. After a few weeks they noticed that a dove had come to live in the eaves of the roof of their house. They were so excited; they took it as a seal of God on their being in Israel. But they noticed that every time they slammed a door the dove would fly away. Every time they had an argument with each other (and began shouting) the dove would fly away. They both feared that maybe one day the dove would fly away and not come back. Sandy said to his wife Bernice, 'Either the dove adjusts to us or we adjust to the dove'. It changed their lives – just to keep that dove near them! And yet the Holy Spirit is a thousand times more sensitive than that!

If we take care to learn from the Holy Spirit through prayer and experience, we not only get to know God's ways; we see how sinful we are. That sinfulness should be sufficient to keep us modest about our spiritual claims. When the Dove comes down and we find it easy to smile, forgive, have joy, not get upset so easily or feel a strong faith, we must remember that it is the Lord – not us – who is the cause of this wonderful feeling. But when the anointing lifts and we find ourselves in the middle of a forest fire – behaving in an embarrassing way – it should teach us never, never, never to be proud of what we are like in ourselves.

The Lord might treat you like Hezekiah, leaving you so as to test you in order to see what is in your heart. Not that *God* learns anything he didn't already know; he lets us see for ourselves what we are like without him. It can be most humbling. But edifying. So the next time you are criticised, let any claim to modesty, meekness or humility be tested by how you take it. If you manage to take severe criticism and can turn the other check, you can perhaps feel pretty good about it – as long as you know God has been merciful to you.

7

SELF-RIGHTEOUSNESS

'The Pharisee stood up and prayed about himself: "God, I thank you that I am not like other men – robbers, evildoers, adulterers – or even like this tax-collector. I fast twice a week and give a tenth of all I get."'

Luke 18:11–12

'I am grateful that I am not as judgmental as all those censorious, self-righteous people around me.'

Anonymous

'Of all bad men religious bad men are the worst.'

C. S. Lewis (1898–1963)

'I believe today that my conduct is in accordance with the will of the Almighty Creator.'

Adolf Hitler (1889–1945)

Some readers may recall the fairly recent account of a man in California who had kidnapped an eleven-year-old girl, held her captive in a little shack in his back yard for his sexual needs for eighteen years. At long last some neighbours reported what they thought was strange activity to the police. When the man was arrested he was actually giving out Christian tracts in the streets. During his trial he apparently had no sense of having done anything wrong. He was apparently self-righteous and smug throughout his trial.

Self-righteousness has a way of blinding us to what we are really like. I have interviewed a number of people over the years who admitted to their dishonesty, sexual promiscuity and stealing (some having been put into prison). Some of these same people will look at you with a straight face and claim they expect to get to heaven because they feel they haven't done anything wrong! Unless the Holy Spirit opens their spiritual eyes, they have no objectivity about themselves. Self-righteousness blinds us to our self-righteousness.

Self-righteousness may be defined as a smug feeling of well-being, whether conscious or unconscious, that comes as a result of justifying ourselves. The conscious feeling comes when we are so sure we are in the right. The unconscious feeling is present when we are not aware that we are arrogant even though we are so sure we are right. Self-righteousness may also be defined as a feeling of smug moral superiority derived from a sense that our beliefs, actions or affiliations are of greater virtue than those of the average person. It is perhaps best known as a 'holier than thou' attitude. It means being piously sure of one's own righteousness.

In this chapter I am treating what happens to be, almost certainly, my own greatest weakness.

Examples of my own folly

I reluctantly share the following story but do so with an acute sense of shame. A few years ago Louise and I were walking along Fifth Avenue in New York City. We noticed a black limousine stopping within a few feet of us and – lo and behold – Senator Edward F. Kennedy got out. He walked toward us, nodded and said, 'How are you?' When I did not put out my hand he just kept walking. It gives me no great pleasure to report this but I do so if only to demonstrate a personal illustration of my own self-righteousness. Why did I not shake Teddy Kennedy's hand? He was never one of my favourite people. I resented his political views as well as what seemed true about his personal life. But when I watched the proceedings of his funeral – which I took the time to view (it lasted for hours), I felt convicted that I had been so smug. I felt so ashamed that I did not reach out my hand that day. Louise felt at the time I should have done so. I now wish I had. It could have resulted in a decent conversation – and who knows what that could have led to? But no. I was too self-righteous to think beyond what was decent and honourable.

You might like to know that my original proposed title for this book was 'The Sin No One Admits to – Self-righteousness', but my publisher felt it would have minimal marketing appeal, so we changed 'self-righteousness' to 'pride'. Nevertheless, the theme of this chapter is actually the one I had in mind for the book all along.

I recall taking a psychological test at the Narramore Christian Foundation in Rosemead, California in May 1970. My church in Fort Lauderdale had paid my way to go there for a month to learn more about Christian counselling. When I arrived I learned that they would teach me to counsel others by counselling *me*. I needed it. On the first day I took a battery of psychological tests. One of the questions was to fill out a sentence beginning with 'I hate ...' My answer was that I hate pharisaical self-righteousness. The irony is, I hated what I am most guilty of!

Why is this chapter important?

Pride is the essential ingredient in self-righteousness. Self-righteousness is the inevitable fruit of pride, not to mention the most obnoxious. But we need also to see the subtlety of self-righteousness. We need to see how it is a part of us and we are not aware of it – as in both cases I described concerning myself above. Perhaps *others* would have noticed it in me, but I was blind to it. This is the thing about self-righteousness; it is easy to see in others but not in ourselves.

The person who thinks they are not self-righteous has no objectivity about themselves – at least not for the moment. The ability to stand above or apart from ourselves is not readily done, and self-righteousness is blinding and therefore keeps us from seeing ourselves.

> 'O wad some Pow'r the giftie gie us
> To see oursels as ithers see us!'
>
> Robert Burns (1759–1796)

We need to see the dangers of self-righteousness, that it is not only repulsive to others but to God. Why is it so dangerous? It is divisive. And it is extremely difficult to see in ourselves. 'I can't help it if I happen to be right' may be our honest opinion. But we become unteachable. The self-righteous person is the most difficult person in the world to reach. When Paul talks about a brother being overtaken in a sin and our need to 'restore such an one in the spirit of meekness; considering thyself, lest thou also be tempted' (Galatians 6:1 KJV), what if that sin is self-righteousness? It is far easier to approach the person who has fallen over some immoral deed than the self-righteous person. Self-righteousness makes us so defensive. Most of all, self-righteousness grieves the Holy Spirit.

I hope this chapter will help us see self-righteousness in ourselves and, as much as possible, overcome it. We must learn the signs, the danger signals. As I said above regarding the time lapse between sin and repentance, so here: we must make every effort to close the gap between the emergence and discovery of our own self-righteousness. But for some it is never discerned at all. For others it may be detected early on, like the beginnings of cancer. And yet one is never eradicated of this disease; we must fight it every day of our lives.

Self-righteousness is frequently the cause of marriage break-down as well as tensions in other human relationships, including in the church. It is because we all stick to our guns and dig in our heels which makes the trouble worse. We need to learn to climb down and admit to being self-righteous.

Self-righteousness is one of the greatest obstacles to true spirituality. There is no doubt that all the works of the flesh militate against walking in the Spirit (Galatians 5:19–26). But self-righteousness is in some ways worse than the most blatant sins of the flesh. Immorality, for example, is an obvious sin and one that brings great disgrace upon the church. But self-righteousness, because it is so blinding, allows for a smugness of spirit to emerge and causes us to be judgmental.

Examples of self-righteousness

Judging others

Being judgmental is a prime example of being self-righteous. 'Do not judge, or you too will be judged. For in the same way you judge others, you will be judged, and with the measure you use, it will be measured to you' (Matthew 7:1–2). It is what makes us point the finger. The prophet Isaiah exhorted us to 'do away with the yoke of oppression, with the pointing finger and malicious talk' (Isaiah 58:9). There is the innate feeling in us that we are competent to judge. It stems from the feeling that we are OK, others are not.

Being judgmental often refers to another's motives. But this is God's prerogative. We are not allowed by the Holy Spirit to offer opinions on the motives or spiritual state of others, however clear such may seem to us. 'Therefore judge nothing before the appointed time; wait till the Lord comes. He will bring to light what is hidden in darkness and will expose the motives of men's hearts. At that time each will receive his praise from God' (1 Corinthians 4:5).

Over twenty years ago I felt convinced that I should read Luke 6:37 every day – literally every day, preferably at the beginning of the day. I have been doing it since and I manage to do it approximately five days out of seven:

> 'Do not judge, and you will not be judged. Do not condemn, and you will not be condemned. Forgive, and you will be forgiven.'
>
> Luke 6:37

Reading this daily has done me no harm. Has it cured me of all my pointing the finger? No. Then why should I do it? It is because by reading it daily I am frequently kept from the unguarded comment that could be a spark that sets a forest on fire. I can tell you categorically that it has helped me immensely. You might try it too. It is part of the 'total forgiveness' package.

Being defensive

Another example of self-righteousness is defensiveness. The greatest freedom is having nothing to prove. Where the Spirit of the Lord is, there is freedom (2 Corinthians 3:17). When we are left to ourselves, there is a need to prove ourselves. When the Dove has come down and we are filled with the Spirit, that need to prove ourselves vanishes. Whenever we begin to defend ourselves we invariably point to the righteousness of our deeds, decisions, stance or conduct. Our being defensive violates the promise that God will do the defending (Romans 12:19). When we try to vindicate ourselves we have moved in on His territory by which we ignored a warning 'No trespassing allowed'.

Being argumentative

Self-righteousness often leads us to being argumentative. 'Now we know that whatever the law says, it says to those who are under the law, so that every mouth may be silenced and the whole world held accountable to God' (Romans 3:19). Being argumentative springs from a hostile spirit, even if it is repressed, which tends to be critical and fault-finding. 'What causes fights and quarrels among you? Don't they come from your desires that battle within you?' (James 4:1). Repression is a defence mechanism that makes us deny what we really feel and is often done unconsciously. Many people have hostile feelings but manage to cover over them by a smile.

Smugness

We have seen the words 'smug' and 'smugness' often in this book. It is best depicted by Jesus when he said to the church of the

Laodiceans, known for being lukewarm. 'You say, "I am rich; I have acquired wealth and do not need a thing". But you do not realise that you are wretched, pitiful, poor, blind and naked' (Revelation 3:17). Smugness is a feeling of self-righteousness whereby one does not merely 'think' but *knows* he or she has got it right and is a cut above others. A person like this seldom analyses their feelings or considers how they appear to others. Some would no doubt be horrified if they suddenly realised how smug they are. The British Special Air Forces rule 'Never complain, never explain, never apologise' sometimes spills over to others who have no mandate to adopt that perspective. The person like this also often wears the mask to cover up deep fears of being found out.

However, when we find ourselves being resentful of smug people we think we know, it could be a fairly strong hint that we are smug too. What we often despise in others is exactly what is so rampant in ourselves. If then I hate the smugness I see in certain people, am I not being smug myself?

Unforgiveness

Holding a grudge is one of the most natural things in the world to sustain. It almost always seems right to do. We feel justified in our hurts. Holding a grudge is not acquired by taking the course 'Ten easy lessons on how to hold a grudge'; it comes from the depth of our hearts without any further learning. 'Out of the *heart* come evil thoughts' – whether they be sexual or a desire for vengeance (Matthew 15:19).

Hanging on to an unforgiving spirit betrays our not having appreciated that we have been forgiven of our own sins and that we have forgotten this. If we *truly* appreciated that we have been forgiven, we would likewise forgive others their trespasses, as the Lord's Prayer puts it (Matthew 6:12). The problem that usually emerges is, we do not feel that we have done anything as bad as the other person; therefore we suppose we are right to blame them, judge them and make them 'pay'. But, like it or not, it is our pride at the bottom of all unforgiveness.

Referring to our good works

The need to call attention to what we have done for the Lord originates in our pride – whether we do this to impress God or those around us. This refers to prayer, giving, fasting, witnessing to the lost, our experiences with God, the gifts we think we have or general faithfulness regarding the church. It also refers to the need to talk about our severe trials and how we dignified them.

I will never forget the day a lady walked to our table in a restaurant in Fort Lauderdale to say she had spent all week visiting people who were house-bound. I commended her. 'What a wonderful thing to do!', I said. She added, 'The joy is in *not telling* it to anybody'. I said, 'But wait a minute. You have just told us'. 'Well', she replied, 'I am only telling you'. But she had already told a dozen! She seemed utterly blind to her problem.

Dale Carnegie in *How to Win Friends and Influence People* claims that the greatest need in the world is the desire to feel important. Some people get their feeling of importance by calling attention to their good works. It is not much different from building a statue to yourself while you are still alive.

How to overcome self-righteousness

It would be a misleading claim to offer hope that one can overcome self-righteousness. It would therefore be unfair if I promised to show how you can be rid of the problem. Like cholesterol in the body, we will always have some – the good and the bad. But the suggestions that follow are designed to help one on a *daily* basis. Like the manna in the desert, there was only enough for a day at a time. Perhaps it will make us just a little more pleasant to live with. But no one should expect to be completely devoid of self-righteousness; only Jesus was like that.

First, we must recognise that self-righteousness is our own problem. It is not *their* problem – it is yours and mine. If we do not see it in ourselves, there is no way forward. If we claim to be without sin – and the essence of this sin is almost always self-righteousness, then we are deceived and the truth is not in us (1 John 1:8). It is one thing to say, 'I know I am not perfect', but that is obvious. Surprise, surprise! This will not shock anybody. But try admitting this to at least *one other person*. For it takes a lot of guts to say, 'My problem is, that I am self-righteous'. We are loath to admit to this.

My old friend Jack Brothers, now in heaven, was a legendary bonefish guide in the Florida Keys. He was an alcoholic, a member of Alcoholics Anonymous, although he had not tasted alcohol for eleven years. He would never say I 'was' an alcoholic, but I 'am' an alcoholic. He had 'broken his anonymity' years before and was open about his problem. He asked me to join him one morning for his meeting with those who came regularly to AA. It was an amazing occasion for me. One after another the people would introduce themselves ... 'I am Jack Brothers and I am an alcoholic' ... 'I am Mary Jones and I am an alcoholic' ... 'I am Bill Smith and I am an alcoholic'. The chief reason for this: admitting to being an alcoholic was – at first – the hardest thing in the world for each of them to do. But once they had the breakthrough, overcoming pride, they found it liberating to admit to being an alcoholic (although most of them were teetotal).

I think it is much like this with admitting to being self-righteous. I am not suggesting that you go around telling everybody, 'I am self-righteous'! But it would do you no harm to admit it to a few – if only those closest to you. When James talked about confessing your sins to one another in order to be healed (James 5:16), he was showing a way forward to be healed – especially if one thought their sickness could be traced to sin. In much the same way I would lovingly suggest that if you are in big trouble at the moment (whatever the relationship), admit to being self-righteous. I don't say it will be easy. But if one wanted to be *healed* I think it would be worth everything to admit to one's malady. So too if you are having critical problems in relationships at the moment, it would do you no harm to say, 'I fear my problem has been that I have been so self-righteous'. If you find this too much to take on board, at least *admit it to yourself*! Be absolutely aware that you are self-righteous and that this is the root of your problem. It is why you point the finger, make the unguarded comment and find it hard to maintain peace. It is all about pride. So at least admit it to yourself: 'I am self-righteous.' After all, you are!

Second, refuse to compute the wrong done to you. By this I mean do not let their wrongdoing go into your 'computer' – your mind, your memory. Love keeps no record of wrongs (1 Corinthians 13:5). You cannot forget what they did, and this is not what is required. Neither must you live in denial. You will always know what they did. But not to 'compute' it means *not to make a note of it* so you can refer to it later. Love will not keep a record of wrongs. Why do we keep records? To prove we have paid. We do we keep a record of wrongs? So we can say, 'I will remember that' – and sadly we do, and it gets us into big trouble. The way forward is to refuse to compute their injustice; absolutely forgive them on the spot. You don't tell them that of course, but you do it in your heart. Yes. This will help you to overcome pointing the finger and not let any self-righteousness get you into difficulty.

Third, avoid any kind of negative comments. Negative is anything that is critical, judgmental and not designed to bring the good feeling. Avoiding all negative talk is hard. But most negativism springs from an unhappy, worried and self-righteous person wanting to 'spout off' abut this or that. 'Everyone should be quick to listen, slow to speak and slow to become angry' (James 1:19). Problems that flow from self-righteousness do not get off the ground until the tongue takes over (James 3:3–8). When something negative comes to mind – however right it seems at the time to express your opinion, *don't speak.* If you avoid saying what is on your mind – which also may be absolutely true – you will avoid a forest fire. You will never be sorry you held your tongue. If you don't say a single word, no hell will have the opportunity to break out. But when we speak a word that flows from the bitter fountain of self-righteousness, the devil gets in (James 3:11–15).

Fourth, refuse to clear your name. 'Do not take revenge, my friends, but leave room for God's wrath, for it is written: "It is mine to avenge; I will repay", says the Lord' (Romans 12:19). Vindicating is an enterprise that only God is allowed to engage in. What is more, do not deprive God from doing what He does best! All that

God does is good, and it is perhaps superfluous to say that there is such a thing as God doing what he does 'best'. But if there is such a thing it is *vindicating* us. Watch Him do it! But only to the degree you don't try to help Him out! This means: do not speak, do not say a word, do not lift a little finger to make yourself look good. Leave everything to Him.

Live by faith alone in waiting for the outcome of how God will clear your name. 'Therefore judge nothing before the appointed time; wait till the Lord comes. He will bring to light what is hidden in darkness and will expose the motives of men's hearts. At that time each will receive his praise from God' (1 Corinthians 4:5). 'Since ancient times no one has heard, no ear has perceived, no eye has seen any God besides you, *who acts on behalf of those who wait for him*' (Isaiah 64:4 my emphasis). Don't try to figure out in advance how God will vindicate. Faith is believing without seeing (Hebrews 11:1). Be willing to understand nothing that is going on at the time (Proverbs 3:5). His ways of bringing things to pass are 'beyond tracing out' (Romans 11:33). In a word: say nothing, do nothing whatever to assist God so that what He does will be to His glory alone.

The fringe benefits of trying to overcome self-righteousness

We should want to overcome self-righteousness if only because it is so obnoxious to everyone. But it is worth examining what it is like to the degree we overcome self-righteousness.

First, great peace will flow through us. When peace is absent, something is wrong. The un-grieved Spirit is recognisable by peace. Second, the absence of judgmentalism. Third, pleasantness. We feel pleasant and we are pleasant to live with! Fourth, people will seek you out. Self-righteousness repels, but the more you are like Jesus the more people will want to be around you and seek your counsel. Fifth, we begin to love people. Sixth, God will become more real to us and fresh insights into Scripture will emerge.

All efforts to overcome self-righteousness are not easy. But it is the best way to live.

8

SELF-PITY

'Surely in vain have I kept my heart pure; in vain have I washed my hands in innocence. All day long I have been plagued; I have been punished every morning.'
     Psalm 78:13–14

'Why, O Lord, do you reject me and hide your face from me? . . . You have taken my companions and loved ones from me; darkness is my closest friend.'
     Psalm 88:14, 18

'Self-pity is our worst enemy and if we yield to it, we can never do anything wise in this world.'
     Helen Keller (1880–1968)

Self-pity comes naturally to all of us. It is the twin of self-righteousness; they two go together and are often inseparable. We have all fallen into self-pity. Some are more prone to this than others. This may be due to one's temperament and background – or childhood experiences. The psalmist said, 'From my youth I have been afflicted and close to death' (Psalms 88:15). You can be sure too that Satan will take advantage of any weakness in us and usually does not have to look far for self-pity in us. Sooner or later we all find ourselves in this state.

Self-pity has sometimes been linked to what is called the 'dark night of the soul'. It sets in when God hides his face. 'How long,

O Lord? Will you forget me forever? How long will you hide your face from me?' (Psalms 13:1). 'For troubles without number surround me; my sins have overtaken me, and I cannot see. They are more than the hairs of my head, and my heart fails within me' (Psalms 40:12).

Self-pity is feeling sorry for yourself. It is a feeling of sorrow (often self-indulgent) over your own sufferings. It is the psychological state of an individual in perceived adverse situations who has not accepted the situation and – in some cases – does not seem to have the confidence or the ability to cope with it. Like self-righteous people who are quite unteachable, so those afflicted with self-pity we are hard to reach when others want to help them.

Two differences between self-righteousness and self-pity

There are two important differences between self-righteousness and self-pity. First, self-righteousness is a condition into which we are born; it is an essential part of original sin. But self-pity is a choice. We may have not chosen the circumstances that brought us to feel sorry for ourselves, and yet it is a choice we make when we engage in self-pity. We tend to justify self-pity in any case. The second difference follows: whereas we cannot completely overcome self-righteousness we can overcome self-pity. We may not like to believe this, but it is true. We have no excuse to remain in this state. Because self-pity, unlike self-righteousness, is a choice; we can choose to get out of this pit.

Also like self-righteousness, self-pity is a sin. It will not do to blame one's own temperament, personality or circumstances. Not only that; self-pity is at its root often anger directed toward God. We feel sorry for ourselves because God allowed a situation to happen that makes no sense. We feel sorry for ourselves because God seems to have deserted us and there seems to be no way out.

Self-pity is often sulking before God, almost demanding that he either explain himself or immediately give us relief. However, sulking gets us nowhere with God. I wish it did, because if self-pity moved God's heart I would have been favoured countless times!

But it doesn't work to sulk before Him. 'For the wrath of man worketh not the righteousness of God' (James 1:20 KJV). I'm sorry, but as long as we sulk, he backs off; when we humble ourselves, he draws nigh. That is the way it works.

Self-righteousness rears its ugly head when we start claiming that what has happened to us is unfair, that we did not deserve the bad treatment. Self-pity is often also a case of not forgiving ourselves – a form of self-righteousness. It is focusing on ourselves. If we admit to God's forgiveness but do not forgive ourselves, it is because we are not content with His forgiveness but are trying, even if unconsciously, to atone for our folly in some other way.

Why is this subject important?

We all know what it is to wallow in self-pity. It is perhaps good to know we are not alone! But we must not forget this important verse (the first verse any new Christian should memorise): 'No temptation has seized you except what is common to man. And God is faithful; he will not let you be tempted beyond what you can bear. But when you are tempted, he will also provide a way out so that you can stand up under it' (1 Corinthians 10:13). Satan will say to us: 'You are the only one to experience this. God has forgotten you'. He is a liar.

This chapter should also help us better to understand ourselves. Socrates' (469–399 BC) philosophy summed up: 'Know yourself'. The Bible alone leads us to true self-understanding.

As in the case of self-righteousness, we need also to see the subtlety of the sin of self-pity. It moves in without our being aware of it. We need to see that it is often nothing but anger toward God and that it is self-righteousness. It is self-centredness. But it is also unbelief, as when we accuse God of forgetting us.

We will see also in this study that the best of God's servants have experienced self-pity. I find this so encouraging. It is great relief to know that God's sovereign vessels have had this problem.

The best news: we can overcome self-pity. If others have done, so can we.

Biblical examples

Jacob

One of the greatest examples of self-pity was the father of the twelve sons of Israel. Jacob was always focusing upon himself. When he concluded that Joseph had been torn to pieces by some wild animal, he felt sorry for himself and refused help from them. 'All his sons and daughters came to comfort him, but he refused to be comforted. "No", he said, "in mourning will I go down to the grave to my son"' (Genesis 37:35).

One way to identify that we are giving in to self-pity is that we don't accept help. When we prefer to wallow in melancholy rather than accept a way out, it shows we have chosen self-pity as the way forward. How sad! A distinguishing mark of self-pity is unteachableness. This became apparent also when Jacob would not let his sons go to Egypt to buy corn without his son Benjamin. He said, 'My son [Benjamin] will not go down there with you; his brother is dead and he is the only one left. If harm comes to him on the journey you are taking, you will bring my grey head down to the grave in sorrow' (Genesis 42:38). In other words, when there was a way forward Jacob blamed others rather than listen to them. Self-pity was so permeated in Jacob that he was unthinkably insensitive to his sons. Benjamin was *not* the only one left; there were ten others! Jacob became so defensive that he was ready to blame them for his never-ending sorrow.

Joseph

Jacob's favourite son Joseph was put into prison after being falsely accused of trying to rape Potiphar's wife. He was indeed innocent. But self-pity set in. While in prison the Pharaoh's cupbearer and baker were put there. Joseph interpreted their dreams. They indicated that the baker would be hanged in three days (he was), but Joseph could see that the cupbearer to the king would be restored to his position. Knowing his dream interpretation was one hundred percent correct Joseph said to the cupbearer, 'When all goes well with you, remember me and show me kindness; mention me to Pharaoh and get me out of this prison. For I was forcibly carried off from the land of the Hebrews, and even here I have done nothing to deserve being put in a dungeon' (Genesis 40:14–15).

It was not Joseph's finest hour. It was God who put him there – all a part of the divine strategy. This would mean only God would set him free. But Joseph saw a way forward which to him meant he should help God along in the process. Wrong. I think God said, 'Oh Joseph, you should not have said that to the cupbearer. I think you need a couple more years'! But it was during that time that Joseph came to experience total forgiveness. Joseph had to forgive his brothers for their wrong. He had to forgive Jacob for showing favouritism. He had to forgive Potiphar's wife for her false accusation and to forgive Potiphar for believing her. What is more, he even had to forgive God. Not that God had done anything wrong, but God let all this happen.

There comes a time, then, when we even have to forgive God – that is, set him free in our hearts of any blame for what was allowed. Joseph had to wait until no one but God could step in and change things.

Moses

Moses had focused on the negative. It was part of his preparation to overcome a negative spirit. He had challenged God's wisdom in choosing him. He lamented his lack of gifts. He 'said to the Lord, "I have never been eloquent, neither in the past nor since you have spoken to your servant. I am slow of speech and tongue".' So 'Moses said, "'Oh Lord, please send someone else to do it"' (Exodus 4:10, 13). He complained over the slowness of results. '"O Lord, why have you brought trouble upon this people? Is this why you sent me? Ever since I went to Pharaoh to speak in your name, he has brought trouble upon this people, and you have not rescued your people at all"' (Exodus 5:22–23).

King David

David was an example of self-pity before and after he became king. After running from King Saul for so long, he came to the conclusion he would never make it – despite the oath given to him by God. 'But David thought to himself, "One of these days I shall be destroyed by the hand of Saul. The best thing I can do is to escape to the land of the Philistines. Then Saul will give up searching for me anywhere in Israel, and I will slip out of his hand"' (1 Samuel 27:1). Despite being anointed by Samuel (1 Samuel 16:13), David had virtually given up.

There was almost certainly a touch of self-pity over the initial failure to bring the Ark to Jerusalem (2 Samuel 6:9–10). But the lowest point in David's life in this connection was the way he blamed himself for Absalom's death. 'He went up to the room ... and wept. ... '"O my son Absalom! My son, my son Absalom! If only I had died instead of you – O Absalom, my son, my son!"' (2 Samuel 18:33). His mourning was out in the open. But Joab rebuked him – and turned David around – lest David's self-pity cause all his people to forsake him (2 Samuel 19:7). This is the perfect example how overcoming self-pity is an act of the will.

Naaman

Naaman was a high-ranking officer in Syria's military, but he was a leper. He was told by an Israeli servant girl that if he would go to Israel and seek out Elisha the prophet, his leprosy would be healed. Naaman believed her and made his way to Israel. But he was not prepared for the initial welcome. Instead of being warmly welcomed by the prophet, 'Elisha sent a messenger to say to him, "Go, wash yourself seven times in the Jordan, and your flesh will be restored and you will be cleansed"' (2 Kings 5:10).

This word did not at first bless Naaman, who no doubt was an arrogant man. He 'went away angry and said, "I thought that he would surely come out to me and stand and call on the name of the Lord his God, wave his hand over the spot and cure me of my leprosy. Are not Abana and Pharpar, the rivers of Damascus, better than any of the waters of Israel? Couldn't I wash in them and be cleansed?" So he turned and went off in a rage' – of self-pity.

But one of his servants spoke sense to him, persuading Naaman to take Elisha's word seriously. Naaman humbled himself and did just that – and was miraculously healed (2 Kings 5:11–14). This is a good illustration of Isaiah's word: '"For my thoughts are not your thoughts, neither are your ways my ways", declares the Lord' (Isaiah 55:8).

Mary and Martha

Jesus deliberately let Lazarus, the brother of Mary and Martha, die. They had sent word to Jesus, fully persuaded He would stop what He was doing and come straight to Bethany to keep Lazarus from dying. But Jesus showed up four days after the funeral. When Martha heard that Jesus was coming, she went out to meet Him. '"Lord," Martha said to Jesus, "if you had been here, my brother would not have died"' (John 11:21). This was virtually charging Jesus with letting her brother die. Mary was, if anything, angrier. She did not join Martha when she knew Jesus was coming to Bethany; she stayed at home. But Jesus kindly asked for Mary, who got up quickly to meet him (John 11:20, 28–29). She said the same thing to Jesus, '"Lord, if you had been here, my brother would not have died".'

But Jesus soon revealed his strategy in letting Lazarus die; raising him from the dead was a better idea (John 11:17–44). This is another example that God's ways are higher than our ways.

Martha showed a bit of self-pity when she complained that Mary was sitting at Jesus' feet while Martha was doing all the work. 'Lord, don't you care that my sister has left me to do the work by myself? Tell her to help me!' Then came the reply, 'Martha, Martha, you are worried and upset about many things, but only one thing is needed. Mary has chosen what is better, and it will not be taken away from her' (Luke 10:40–42).

All of these accounts indicate that there is a sovereign strategy designed carefully by God when any of us feel sorry for ourselves. I find this so encouraging. God had a plan for each of these people. He has a plan for you too; it is all a part of predesigned purpose.

Further observations

Self-pity itself is counter-productive. It doesn't do any good and gets us nowhere. It never achieves its goals; we only hurt ourselves. Jacob seemed willing to let his family die rather than urge them to do the right thing and go to Egypt where they could buy some food. Job, seen in an earlier chapter, only made himself look more ridiculous by being so defensive. David appeared more willing to pander his sorrow than to be the strong leader he was. Naaman risked missing one of the great miracles of all time.

Self-pity gives the devil a greater opportunity to walk over us and defeat us. The devil loves it when we feel sorry for ourselves. It makes his job easier, being the 'accuser of our brothers' (Revelation 12:10). The devil's aim is to get us to grieve the Holy Spirit. It is one thing to feel sorry for ourselves, but it is worse to verbalise it unless we are confessing it as a shameful sin. If we are complaining, it is sin. If however we are confessing it as something we are sorry about, it is the way forward to being set free.

A convenience

Self-pity is a convenience to avoid responsibility. It is self-defeating, keeping us in a rut. It is self-deceiving, giving us a feeling that we are quite right to be in this state. It is a convenient way of reasoning with ourselves by which we tell ourselves there is no way out! To choose to feel sorry for ourselves is to follow a voice that says, 'What's the use?' That is the devil speaking.

'Do you want to get well?'

There was a man who lay beside the pool of Bethesda for thirty-eight years. It was alleged that if the waters stirred the first person that jumped into the pool got healed. Jesus came alongside and 'he asked him, "Do you want to get well?"' That is an interesting question. Surely the answer would be yes! But no. The man's reply: '"Sir, I have no one to help me into the pool when the water is stirred. While I am trying to get in, someone else goes down ahead of me" (John 5:2–7). This man had the most convenient excuse ever! It was a convenience that lasted thirty-eight years. Self-pity is more interested in defending itself than looking for a solution. We don't want our problems solved; we want them understood.

Self-pity is a choice we make. Jacob 'refused to be comforted' (Genesis 37:35). He made a choice. The thing about self-pity sadly is that we tend to welcome it rather than resist it. It is not a condition over which we have no control. It is a choice. It is often a choice made in anger. Faith says: there is a reason God let this happen.

Overcoming self-pity

First, recognise self-pity as a sin. This means it needs to be confessed and repented of. Once we see this as a sin we have no option but to deal with it. As long as we see it as a temperamental weakness, we will excuse it every time – and be in the same condition five or ten or thirty-eight years later! The good news is this: 'If we confess our sins [Jesus Christ] is faithful and just to forgive us our sins, and to cleanse us from all unrighteousness' (1 John 1:9 KJV). It is not a bad idea, as in the case of self-righteousness, to confess this to another person, because when you take that remarkable step you are saying, 'I am ashamed of it and I want to do something about it'.

Second, listen to those who want to help you. At the pool of Bethesda, 'Jesus said to [the man], "Get up! Pick up your mat and walk." The man listened, obeyed and "was cured; he picked up his mat and walked"' (John 5:8–9). Had Jacob listened to his sons, God may have begun to speak to him as in former days. It would be another twenty-two years before Jacob had further communication with God (Genesis 46:1–2). 'Wounds from a friend can be trusted' (Proverbs 27:6 NIV 2011).

I myself was wallowing in self-pity when an old friend – Josif Tson – said: 'R.T., you must totally forgive them; until you totally forgive them you will be in chains.' It was the hardest but kindest word I ever heard. Listening to Josif turned out to be my finest hour in twenty-five years at Westminster Chapel.

Third, admit that you are no better off to continue in this state. Recognise that it is a cul-de-sac – self-defeating and self-deceiving! You are only hurting yourself. Things will not change until you snap out of it. Self-pity is a choice; overcoming it is a choice.

Helen Keller was the first deaf and blind person to earn a B.A. degree. She did it largely by overcoming self-pity. She said that to give in to it guaranteed you would never do anything 'wise'. She refused to yield to it and became one of the most remarkable human beings in human history. If she could do it, so can you.

Don't merely pray about it; do it!

9

HYPOCRISY

'So when you give to the needy, do not announce it with trumpets, as the hypocrites do in the synagogues and on the streets, to be honoured by men. I tell you the truth, they have received their reward in full.'
Matthew 6:2

'Everything they do is done for men to see.'
Matthew 23:5

'The greatest way to live with honour in this world is to be what we pretend to be.'
Socrates (469–399 BC)

'When you say you agree with a thing in principle you mean that you have not the slightest intention of carrying it out in practice.'
Otto von Bismarck (1815–1898)

'I like your Christ, I do not like your Christians. Your Christians are so unlike your Christ.'
Mahatma Gandhi (1869–1948)

In my early days at Westminster Chapel there was a man (though he has been in heaven for many years, I will call him Dan) who befriended us, paid for our holidays in America, took us to the best restaurants in London and thought I was the best thing to come to the church in Britain in years. I will never forget an evening Louise and I had with him and his wife at a restaurant in Shepherd's Bush, West London. He had just returned from Los Angeles. The Southern Baptist Convention was, by coincidence, meeting in Los Angeles at the time. Dan decided to attend it one evening when the speaker happened to be Arthur Blessitt (the man who has carried a cross literally all over the world – holding the Guinness Book of Records for the world's longest walk). Dan was bubbling over with excitement from Arthur's talk. He seemed to quote Arthur word for word. One of Arthur's comments was something like this: '"Will Los Angeles be any different after 25,000 Southern Baptists have come to town? How many of you will witness to these people? How many people in Los Angeles will be saved as a result of all of you being here?"' Dan was moved almost to tears. So was I.

I had met Arthur twice at that time. Once was at a Southern Baptist rally in Miami in 1969, the other was in London in 1980. As it was a Friday I invited him to hear me speak that night at our Bible study. At the end of the study I said, '"I will always wonder what it would have been like for Arthur Blessitt to speak at Westminster Chapel. Arthur, come up here and take ten minutes to greet the people".' He came up, took about an hour – he mesmerised the people. It was an important evening for all of us, especially Louise and me.

In the meantime I was voted to be president of the Fellowship of Independent Evangelical Churches (FIEC). We were discussing who should be the closing speaker at the annual meeting of the FIEC the next year which, as it happened, was to be held in Westminster Chapel. Having just been with Dan at that restaurant a few weeks before, I suggested Arthur Blessitt. They thought I was joking. It took three committee meetings before they finally agreed. I will never forget that evening as long as I live. The placed was filled to overflowing. Just before we walked up to the pulpit Arthur said something about the 'invitation' he would give. 'Invitation? Arthur, we don't do that here.' 'We don't?' he asked. 'Well,' I said, 'if you feel led, go ahead.' He replied, I can tell you right now I do.' He did.

Arthur preached for an hour on 'Why do we still need the cross?' It was electrifying. He gave an appeal for people to stand up (in front of everybody) if they needed to be saved. As best as I recall about eighty people stood, including Beryl Denton, our daughter Melissa's best friend – who years later became my secretary. Beryl was gloriously saved that night.

For the next several days I had fire in my bones like I had never experienced in my life. I wondered what would it take to get Arthur to spend a month at Westminster Chapel? I was able to persuade him. He preached five Sunday nights during the month of May 1982 (I took the Sunday mornings). But after the second week he got us out on the streets – to witness to anybody who happened to be there. I was now forced to go outside my comfort zone. I had never done anything like it in my life.

I will pass over a lot of interesting details only to reveal that this is when I felt the call of the Holy Spirit to start our Pilot Light ministry. On the first Saturday in June 1982 – after Arthur moved on, our Pilot Light Ministry was born. I was so full of zeal that I would have gone out *alone* if nobody joined me, although six people did. It is a ministry that continues to this day – including other places in the world. Only God knows how many people will be in heaven as a consequence of that street ministry – done every Saturday morning fifty-two weeks a year except Christmas and Boxing Day.

The high-water mark of our Farewell Service in Westminster Chapel in January 2002 was when Charlie Stride, a Pilot Light convert, gave his testimony. By taking Arthur Blessitt seriously my own ministry was transformed. I devote an entire chapter to him in my book *In Pursuit of His Glory*. The best single decision I made in twenty-five years at Westminster Chapel was to invite Arthur. It would not have happened had not Dan come back from Los Angeles with his glowing report of Arthur's preaching.

But there is one more ingredient that makes the purpose of this scenario complete. My friend Ed Stetzer says, 'Christians love evangelism as long as someone else is doing it'. As it happened, my friend Dan lived within walking distance of the

Chapel. Whereas you would have thought he would join us on the streets in evangelising Westminster where he lived – having been so stirred up by Arthur in Los Angeles, instead he wasted no time in distancing himself overnight from Louise and me. The paid holidays in America stopped. The invitations to five-star restaurants stopped. He even stopped coming to hear me preach. Apparently it was good for Arthur to tell Southern Baptists what to do. It was good if they tried to save Los Angeles. But when we tried to do the exact same thing in London? Oh dear. The irony is, had not Dan reported about Arthur's preaching to Southern Baptists as he did, there would be no Pilot Light Ministry in Westminster today. Dan was a good man and a great blessing to our family for a while. We spent many hours bonefishing in the Florida Keys. He loved my theology. And yet he is quite typical of church members everywhere. They will send money to save the souls of Nigeria, China or India. They will pay for the Arthur Blessitts of this world to evangelise the lost. As Ed Stetzer says, they love evangelism as long as someone else is doing it.

I don't mean to be unfair, but are you any different? When is the last time you talked to one other person about their soul? When is the last time you led a soul to Jesus Christ?

Here are some words of from C. T. Studd, who founded the Heart of Africa Mission:

> 'Only one life, 'twill soon be past;
> Only what's done for Christ will last.'

* * *

'If Jesus Christ be God and died for me, then no sacrifice can be too great for me to make for him.'

* * *

> 'Some want to live within the sound of church or chapel bell;
> I want to run a rescue shop within a yard of hell.'

* * *

'Let us not glide through this world and then slip quietly in to heaven, without having blown the trumpet loud and long for our

Redeemer, Jesus Christ. *Let us see to it that the devil will hold a thanksgiving service in hell, when he gets the news of our departure from the field of battle.'*

C. T. Studd (1860–1931)

My old friend Rolfe Barnard had a sermon called 'The Man who was Known in Hell', based upon this passage:

> 'Some Jews who went around driving out evil spirits tried to invoke the name of the Lord Jesus over those who were demon-possessed. They would say, "In the name of Jesus whom Paul preaches, I command you to come out". Seven sons of Sceva, a Jewish chief priest, were doing this. The evil spirit answered them "Jesus I know, and Paul I know about, but who are you?"'

Acts 19:13–15

The point of Rolfe's sermon was, 'I want to be known in hell. They knew about Paul, they knew about Jesus. Have they heard of me?' Sadly most of us are no threat to the devil. But to be a threat to Satan is costly. It may cost you everything you have – your reputation, possessions, friends, job or comfort. Do you want to be known in hell? I certainly do.

Definition of hypocrisy

The word 'hypocrite' (Gr. *hupokrites*) is used twenty times in the New Testament, mostly by Jesus. In the ancient Greek language it meant 'actor'. But as the word developed it came to be used in a negative sense. Philo (20 BC–AD 50) and Josephus (AD 37–100) generally used the word in a pejorative sense. And so did Jesus. The word translated 'hypocrisy' is used seven times in the New Testament. The meaning then and now comes to this, describing a person who pretends to be what he is not.

Why would a person do this? Our pride. We want the bouquet from people for having *appeared* to be something. One does this because he or she does not have it on their radar screen to seek the praise that comes from God only; they want the glory from one another (John 5:44).

Have you any idea how *little* the praise of men will mean to you at the Judgment Seat of Christ? It will not only mean nothing to you; you will disdain it. You will be embarrassed by it. You would give a thousand worlds had you not regarded the opinions of people so highly. We used to sing this hymn at the Chapel:

> 'Go, labour on! 'tis not for naught;
> Thy earthly loss is heavenly gain;
> Men heed thee, love thee, praise thee not;
> The Master praises: what are men?'

> Horatius Bonar (1808–89)
> Ananias and Sapphira

Here is a couple that became a part of the earliest church. They were right in the middle of all that was going on. Except for one thing: while others were selling their property and bringing *all* the money to the apostles (to be distributed to the poor), Ananias and Sapphira sold a piece of property but kept back part of the money for themselves. Their sin was greed combined with a need to make everyone around them think they too had brought all their money to the apostles. They would not have sinned had they not sold their property; their sin was selling it and *claiming* to bring all the money to the apostles. There is no scriptural mandate that hints they should have sold their property. But they wanted to be *seen* as having done this. In non-revival times they would have got away with this; nobody would have discerned a thing. But there was so much Holy Spirit power present that hypocrisy was picked up on Peter's radar screen at once. 'Peter said, "Ananias, how is it that Satan has so filled your heart that you have lied to the Holy Spirit and have kept for yourself some of the money you received for the land? ... You have not lied to men but to God." When Ananias heard this, he fell down and died. And great fear seized all who heard what had happened' (Acts 5:3–5). The same thing followed three hours later with Sapphira who, following her husband, lied.

'At that moment she fell down at his feet and died.... Great fear seized the whole church and all who heard about these events' (Acts 5:7–11).

They were judged by the Holy Spirit. 'When we are judged by the Lord, we are being disciplined so that we will not be condemned with the world' (1 Corinthians 11:32). Their hypocrisy did not mean they were not saved and, as I said, would have gone unnoticed in a non-revival situation. I fear there have been countless thousands since who have lied to God and who continued on as if nothing happened.

Peter's hypocrisy

But according to Paul, this same Peter who exposed the hypocrisy of Ananias and Sapphira was later guilty of hypocrisy himself. This was when Peter sat and ate with Gentiles – so far, so good – until 'certain men came from James'. These were Jews who were not fully emancipated from the Law of Moses. The moment they arrived Peter excused himself from the Gentiles lest he be seen with them. Peter 'was afraid of those who belonged to the circumcision group. The other Jews joined him in his *hypocrisy*, so that even Barnabas was led astray'. Paul rebuked Peter 'in front of them all' (Galatians 2:11–14 *emphasis* added).

Dear Peter was afraid of what James back in Jerusalem would think. His lack of courage is surprising. Although he would never again deny Jesus as he once did, his behaviour shows that he feared James more than he was prepared to uphold Paul's freedom and theological perspective which signalled a clear break from the Mosaic Law.

Paul was a minority voice in his day. He counselled Timothy, 'do not be ashamed to testify about our Lord, or ashamed of me his prisoner' (2 Timothy 1:8). It would not have been easy to stand with Paul in those days. His theology won out and in his death he received the honour he deserved. We all want to stand beside those we think will be the 'wave of the future' – or already accepted by the majority.

Mahatma Gandhi

We never know who is watching us and who will form opinions about Jesus Christ owing to what they see in us. Every time I go to Durban, South Africa, I think of Mahatma Gandhi. Gandhi began reading the New Testament when in South Africa and was very impressed with Jesus, so much that he seriously considered becoming a Christian. That is, until he met so many Christians that turned him right off Christianity. He had observed members of the Dutch Reformed Church in South Africa, saw their hypocrisy and knew at once that for him being a Christian was not to be a way forward. 'I like your Christ, I do not like your Christians. Your Christians are so unlike your Christ', he said. One could wonder how history could have been changed had Gandhi met a godly person who was both theologically sound but made him think of Jesus.

The Pharisees

Jesus' chief opponents were the Pharisees. They were less prestigious than the Sadducees but far more in number. They were regarded as the most holy of men. But Jesus called them hypocrites – actors – who did everything to be seen of men. They prayed to be seen. They gave to alms to be seen. They fasted to be seen. They truly felt they were superior to everybody when it came to holiness. The fact that Jesus accepted sinners – sat with them, ate with them and even chose Matthew a tax-collector as one of the Twelve – made them feel safer than ever in their opposition to Jesus. In any case, they rejected Jesus because it would not have been politically correct to accept him. Jesus said to them, 'How *can* you believe' – that is how could you, how are you able to believe – 'if you accept praise from one another, yet make no effort to obtain the praise that comes from the only God' (John 5:44 *emphasis* added). If you have wondered why the Jews rejected Jesus as their Messiah, John 5:44 tells you: they were so needful of one another's praise that they did not even consider receiving the praise that comes from God.

This is how the Jews missed their Messiah. It is how many Christians miss the genuine move of God when it is right in front of them. They are so biased that they dismiss out of hand moves of the Spirit that could have set them free. A British couple – missionaries in India – returned to England because they heard revival had broken out in Wales in 1904. Their ship landed at Southampton, then they came up to London. Old friends greeted them. 'What are you doing back in England?' 'Oh', they said, 'we are going to Wales to see the great revival'. 'Don't bother', their friends replied, 'it is Welsh emotionalism'. The couple got on the next ship and returned to India – all because they took the word of some biased believers.

It is vitally important that you and I become gripped by the possibility of receiving the praise that comes from God only – and not the praise of men. The greatest safeguard to hypocrisy is to be governed by wanting God's honour – his opinion and glory – and eschew wanting the approval of people. What is more: a reward at the Judgment Seat of Christ is assured when you live like that.

10

CLIMBING UP, CLIMBING DOWN

'I know both how to be abased, and I know how to abound ...'
Philippians 4:12 KJV

'I am afraid that when I come again my God will humble me before you ...'
2 Corinthians 12:21

'If you have embarrassed yourself and are going to laugh about it some day, you might as well start today.'
Anonymous

'I'm willing to admit that I may not always be right, but I am never wrong.'
Samuel Goldwyn (1882–1974)

You will recall that our definition of being proud is taking yourself too seriously. The person who takes himself too seriously is usually quite defensive and cannot laugh at himself. He or she may have a sense of humour as long as it is laughing at someone else – but never at themselves! And yet – almost certainly – we will one day be able to laugh at ourselves for what was so humbling at first. If you and I can close the time gap between initially being defensive and later laughing at ourselves, it will show some maturity. Why don't we learn to laugh at ourselves now?

None of us likes being humbled however. The Apostle Paul did not relish the possibility of being humbled before the Corinthians, but he was braced for it. What gave him strength was recalling that our Lord 'was crucified in weakness' (2 Corinthians 13:4). Only God knows how much this principle – the willingness to look like a wimp – has meant to me.

It is more fun to climb up than it is to climb down. In Britain (now too in America) it is called 'eating humble pie' – that is, to act submissively, especially when admitting to an error. In America we also call it 'eating crow'.

Climbing down is having to retract what we once said or believed. Though it can be humbling, it is good for the soul! The hardest thing in the world for some of us is to say 'I was wrong'. Someone said that the best way to sustain a happy marriage is to admit you are wrong when you are wrong – but if you are right to keep quiet about it! It is the best way to approach any relationship and it is certainly the right way to be toward God. If you are wrong, confess it; if you are right, realise it is by the sheer grace of God that this is the case.

Climbing up

Climbing up can be understood two ways. First, it could be what God has done for you – being exalted or promoted. It could mean the better job, the better situation, the new friendship or a higher income. When you know that God is behind this it is a wonderful thing. It means you were passive in it all. It is what God did. When we nudge the arm of providence to make something happen, there will always be a doubt if the right thing occurred. Beware of pushing yourself forward, trying to make things happen.

And yet it is not always easy to know when you are doing this. For example, I used to be a door-to-door vacuum cleaner salesman. I was as aggressive as I could possibly be when it came to making a sale. I learned how to get into a home, make a sales pitch and close the deal in a very short period of time. I followed an old axiom a veteran salesman taught me: 'I'd rather sell and regret having sold than keep and regret having kept.'

I have had to be careful here in other ways. Because I learned how to sell a vacuum cleaner to a person who was not the slightest bit in the market for one, I have had to stop myself from pushing too hard in things that belonged entirely to God's prerogative – for example in kingdom matters. Where does one draw the line? Take for example evangelism. I taught Pilot Lights: 'Do your best to lead a person to Christ when you have their attention, as you could be the last person that ever talks to them about Jesus Christ.' Although some of my Calvinist friends have chided me for pushing too hard in this area, I have no regrets. I think of the man who rushed up to the great Charles Spurgeon following his strong evangelistic talk: 'But Mr. Spurgeon, what if we convert one of the non-elect?' Spurgeon patted him on the back and replied, 'God will forgive you for that'. I have never regretted asking a person to close with Christ.

But there are two things that are absolutely forbidden: (1) to promote yourself or (2) to clear your name. These two things are God's prerogative alone. On these two matters always wait for God's time. He is never too late, never too early, but always just on time. It gives me peace when I recall that every single church to which I was called over the past fifty-five years came without my lifting a little finger.

So when God says 'climb up', it is good. It is like Jesus' parable that we should take the lowest seat and wait to be invited to 'come up higher'.

Secondly, climbing up can be a bad thing, as when pride is what motivates you. Take social climbing: a social climber is one who seeks social prominence – or who wants to be seen with important people – sometimes by unsubtle behaviour. He or she often tries to get accepted in a higher social class by being friendly with people who belong to that class. The motivation for this is pride. It is said that a few wealthy Americans in the early 1900s abandoned their Presbyterian faith to become Episcopalians. It was regarded as a step up the social ladder. It is speculative to suggest that this was the motive behind the aforementioned fatal move of Ananias and

Sapphira, but for some reason it was important to them to be seen as being 'in' with the early believers. Peter was certainly 'in the wrong' when he did not want certain Jews to see him eating with Gentiles (Galatians 2:11).

There is nothing wrong with wanting to improve your lot, get a better job, get a better education or improve your living situation. Whereas slaves who were Christians were generally counselled to obey their masters with 'reverence for the Lord' (Colossians 3:22), Paul also said, 'if you can gain your freedom, do so' (1 Corinthians; Corinthians 7:21).

The principle we must not only agree to, but follow is always this: let God do the promoting, the vindicating – in His time.

Climbing down

Climbing down, like climbing up, can also be seen two ways: (1) when we do it voluntarily and humbly; and (2) when we are forced to climb down because we have no other choice.

The prime example of humbling oneself – although it was certainly not a climb down – was when the Second Person of the Godhead decided that He would turn His back on infinite glory and become 'nothing'. Not only that, having become a man, Jesus 'humbled himself and became obedient to death – even death on a cross!' (Philippians 2:8). Moreover, you and I are exhorted to do the same thing: to have this mind like Christ Jesus, 'who, though he was in the form of God, did not count equality with God a thing to be grasped, but emptied himself' (Philippians 2:6–7 ESV). Jesus' example was not a climb down because there was no retraction involved, but we must always emulate Him to the hilt when it comes to you and me needing to humble ourselves.

A major climb down for David – before he was king – was when he vowed to get vengeance upon Nabal who treated David and his men so unfairly. '"Put on your swords!"' (1 Samuel 25:13) David ordered, later swearing an oath: '"May God deal with David, be it ever so severely, if by morning I leave alive one male of all who belong to [Nabal]"' (v. 22). Four hundred of his men headed straight for Nabal. But Nabal's wife Abigail intervened, headed swiftly to plead with David, got off her donkey and fell face down to him and pleaded for him to change his mind (vv. 23–31). Despite his oath, he climbed down and thanked Abigail: 'May you be blessed for your good judgment and for keeping me from bloodshed this day ... I have heard your words and granted your request' (vv. 33–35). Years later, after he became king, David also climbed down humbly from his plan to build the temple and accepted Nathan's verdict that he should give this up.

We turn to the second category, when one has no choice but to climb down. It is not necessarily doing so humbly but because one has no choice.

Jacob had adamantly and stubbornly declared, 'My son [Benjamin] will not go down there with you' (Genesis 42:38); that is, with the ten brothers to Egypt to buy food. Jacob was angry with everybody – full of self-pity – when he made that vow. But the famine worsened. Jacob ordered them to return to Egypt to buy food, but Judah reminded him that the prime minister of Egypt would not negotiate with them unless the other brother showed up with them all. Judah pleaded with his father – then offered to guarantee his safety; 'you can hold me personally responsible for him ... as it is, if we had not delayed, we could have gone and returned twice'. Jacob climbed down. But he really had no choice; it was not an act of humility (Genesis 43:1–15).

The same is true of David when he was full of self-pity regarding Absalom's death. The truth was, David's men had accomplished a big victory. When they were rejoicing, David was weeping. Only Joab could have spoken to the king as he did. '"Today you have humiliated all your men, who have just saved your life and the lives of your sons ... You love those who hate you and hate those who love you. You have made it clear today that the commanders and their men mean nothing to you. I see that you would be pleased if Absalom were alive today and all of us were dead. Now go out and encourage your men. I swear by the Lord that if you don't go out, not a man will be left with you by nightfall. This will be worse for you than all the calamities that have come upon you from your youth till now". Joab's severe reprimand worked. 'So the king got up and took his seat in the gateway' (2 Samuel 19:5–8). David climbed down, but he would have been in far worse shape if he hadn't done so. It was hardly a gracious gesture.

Paul and returning to Jerusalem

One of the more interesting (and debatable) facets of the Apostle Paul's life was regarding his adamant insistence regarding going to Jerusalem over against prophetic warnings not to do so. Paul made up his mind to return to Jerusalem after one of his missionary journeys. Everybody without exception urged him not to do so. Luke (who wrote Acts) seems to be of the opinion that Paul should not have gone. Certain disciples, 'Through the Spirit ... urged Paul not to go on to Jerusalem' (Acts 21:4). Had Luke not put those words 'Through the Spirit', one might have thought Paul was absolutely right, as if Paul could make no mistakes. Not only that: Agabus (to whom Luke refers as having been accurate in his prophecy about an approaching famine, Acts 11:28) warned that Paul would be bound and handed over to the Gentiles by the Jews of Jerusalem (Acts 21:11). Everybody pleaded with Paul not to go (v. 12), but he said, '"I am ready not only to be bound, but also to die in Jerusalem for the name of the Lord Jesus"' (v. 13). Paul stuck to his guns and would not climb down.

What we know is that Paul did not have great success in Jerusalem. When he arrived he was pressured into doing what must have been very distasteful to him: he took a vow to show he was truly a good Jew (Acts 21:20–26), his testimony was violently rejected (Acts 23:9–15ff). Paul was put in prison and eventually went to Rome. Was Paul right or was he wrong? He did not ever climb down, and the nearest he came to commenting on this aspect of his sojourn was when he wrote to the Philippians, 'Now I want you to know, brothers, that what has happened to me has really served to advance the gospel' (Philippians 1:12). But he never climbed down.

Most of us have had to climb down over decisions or opinions we were once so sure of. I made one fairly significant exegetical interpretation of Hebrews 6:4–6 while I was at Westminster Chapel. I used to hold that the people described in that passage were counterfeit believers – that they were never truly converted. I have it in print – see my book *Jonah* (a series of sermons at Westminster Chapel in 1977), my first book. In the summer of 1982 I came to a different view, namely, that the people described in Hebrews 6:4–6 were true believers indeed but that they had become stone deaf to the Holy Spirit – and could not hear God anymore. It did not mean they were eternally lost but that they forfeited any inheritance they could have had. My entire exposition of Hebrews 5:11–6:20 is found in *Are You Stone Deaf to the Spirit or Rediscovering God?*

I mentioned above that I probably left Trevecca prematurely back in 1956. I also became a bit defensive in not finishing my education, not wanting to admit I might not have heard from God in 1956. I also pointed out that the great Charles Spurgeon managed okay without higher education. But I was forced to admit in subsequent years that I was no Spurgeon! It was humbling to return to Trevecca fourteen years later, but it was one of the best decisions I ever made.

But the most public climb down I probably ever made was with regard to the 'Toronto blessing' – a decision that has caused me to lose more support and respect than any decision I can think of. I have told the details elsewhere, as in *The Anointing*. In a word: having said it was not of God – and cautioning the members of Westminster Chapel accordingly, I spoke weeks later from the same pulpit to say that it was of God indeed. Although many doors have closed to me as a result of this stance, I can honestly say I would do the same thing over again. Am I too proud to admit I made a mistake? You decide.

11

CHOOSING YOUR FRIENDS

'"I will celebrate before the Lord. I will become even more undignified than this, and I will be humiliated in my own eyes. But by these slave girls you spoke of, I will be held in honour."'

2 Samuel 6:21–22

'So do not be ashamed to testify about our Lord, or ashamed of me his prisoner. But join with me in suffering for the gospel ...'

2 Timothy 1:8

'Anybody can sympathise with the sufferings of a friend, but it requires a very fine nature to sympathise with a friend's success.'

Oscar Wilde (1854–1900)

'Misfortune shows those who are not really friends.'

Aristotle 384–322 BC)

We are fairly stupid if we choose friends on the basis of what makes us look good. It is well and good if our friends happen to be upstanding people, but if that is a requirement for finding friends, most of us will be bankrupt in that department. A friend is someone who knows all about you and still likes you. He or she is one who not only can weep when you weep but rejoice when you rejoice. I would say therefore a true friend is one who can rejoice with you.

There are of course levels of friendships. Not all those whom you love will you like. Not all those you find helpful and respectful would be those you choose to go on vacation with. Some of those who used to go on vacation with us turned out to be – almost – enemies.

There is nothing like the pure Gospel and obedience to the Holy Spirit to reveal who your true friends are. Not only that; upholding the pure Gospel and maintaining careful obedience to the Holy Spirit is our first priority. It is the same thing as seeking first the kingdom of God and his righteousness (Matthew 6:33), then letting other things – including God choosing your friends – be added. I can testify in my old age that God has picked my friends. I did not try to make a friendship happen; I have been amazed how He did it. Not all those who used to be my close friends are close friends today. The Lord gives, the Lord takes away; He knows the kind of friendships we need – and He will supply them.

When we first began our ministry at Westminster Chapel, we were given the 'rush' by certain people. So many people wanted to be our friends. I suppose I was seen as the wave of the future (or something like that) and we had people coming to us right, left and centre – wanting to spend time with us, eat with us and have our phone number. Only a handful of those people are close friends today. Not because we dropped them; they dropped us! The details would make a best-selling book – but will never be printed!

I only know one thing in this connection. It was two things: (1) the Gospel and (2) our obedience to the Holy Spirit that revealed who our true friends were. Not that all these went on vacation with us, but they certainly proved to be the kind of friendships we needed in our darkest hour. Those friendships abide to this day.

King David found out who his true friends were. One of my favourite sermons out of the year-long series I did in Westminster Chapel on the life of David was called 'Finding your Friends' – based on the account when David managed to bring the Ark of the Covenant into Jerusalem. He was so excited. He had previously failed with this effort. But when he saw this time he would succeed, he got carried away. 'David, wearing a linen ephod, danced before the Lord with all his might, while he and the entire house of Israel brought up the ark of the Lord with shouts and the sound of trumpets' (2 Samuel 6:14–15). It was not what one expected of a dignified king. But this did not matter. David 'lost it'! He went over the top in showing his pleasure that the Ark was coming to Jerusalem. He then sacrificed burnt offerings and fellowship offerings before the Lord. He blessed the people, gave each a loaf of bread, cakes of dates and raisins (vv. 17–19). It was almost certainly the happiest day of his life.

That is, until he returned home. Michal, the daughter of King Saul – who had been given to David to be a wife, was indignant. '"How the king of Israel has distinguished himself today, disrobing in the sight of the slave girls of his servants as any vulgar fellow would"' (2 Samuel 6:20). What a downer for David.

I have had this happen. Certainly not with family, but with those I thought were wanting the honour and glory of God. It happened again and again. When I first had Arthur Blessitt at Westminster Chapel I felt that way. I had the same feeling when Rodney Howard-Browne and John Arnott preached for us. When the presence of God was manifest it was – to me – something worthy of being thrilled about. But sadly not all felt this way. I began to get phone calls. One man stormed out of the service and vowed he would not return until things changed. Some of my closest supporters began to go quiet. When we began the Pilot Light ministry, there were criticisms of the kind of people who were making professions and coming to the Chapel. I began to get reports of one person after another resigning their membership. Those were painful days.

But in the process I found my true friends. Who were they? My true friends were those who rejoiced as I did that the presence of the Holy Spirit was becoming more and more evident. I had thought (perhaps naïvely) that *all* my followers wanted the same thing as I did. But one of my esteemed deacons, observing the upheaval and kind of people we were attracting, said to me, 'Do we really want revival after all?' – by which he meant 'probably not'.

There was another noticeable factor. The kind of people who wanted to become Pilot Lights and join us on the streets, were not the rank and file middle class Brit that had made the Chapel the church it had become. Those not so well dressed or refined outnumbered the more sophisticated and educated people who came out on Saturdays. Not only that: those who were making professions of faith were generally not from the House of Lords nor were they Members of Parliament. They were ordinary, less than middle class, sometimes jobless and homeless people. Many were tourists.

It meant a paradigm shift in the Chapel. Singing choruses along with the old hymns became the norm. I started giving invitations for people to confess Christ publicly. Old supporters were leaving us in droves. Some of those who replaced them reminded me of those who danced with David.

David explained to Michal that it was 'before the Lord' he did this. '"I will celebrate before the Lord"', he stated to her. There is more: '"I will become even more undignified than this, and I will be humiliated in my own eyes. But by these slave girls you spoke of, I will be held in honour"' (2 Samuel 6:21–22). David had found his friends – that is, his true friends. His true friends were those who rejoiced in what he rejoiced; who celebrated what he celebrated and who felt as he did.

This sort of thing reveals who your friends are. It did not only happen to me. Others in the Chapel went through the same thing! Old friendships were challenged. I felt sorry for some of those who suffered being distanced by some of their oldest and best friends. It happened in families too – when fathers and sons were on opposite sides. It brought home one of Jesus' statements: '"For I have come to turn 'a man against his father, a daughter against her mother, a daughter-in-law against her mother-in-law – a man's enemies will be the members of his own household'"' (Matthew 10:35–36).

But there was a wider pain for me in those days. Old friends outside the Chapel distanced themselves from us. Churches where I was previously invited to preach were no longer beckoning for me. Virtually all my invitations to preach in Britain stopped – almost overnight! For nearly two years I had nothing to do from Sunday to Sunday but to prepare sermons. It had been the norm for me to go out all over Britain – at least once or twice a week – to preach.

When I would go to ministers' meetings or fraternals, it was like going to an ice house. People would turn their heads when they saw me. I felt resentment from the same people who once seemed thrilled to have my company. One minister wrote me a letter to rebuke me and said, 'R.T., if revival came to London I'd know it'. But we did not claim that revival came. Not at all.

That was the hard part. The changes we made in those days did not result in filling the Chapel. New people were coming all the time, but they were cautioned by old members: 'There's trouble here, this is not the place you want to come' – and drove people away. We were like a bucket with holes in it; water going in all the time but the bucket did not fill.

Worse still was when friendships in America were strained. It was important for some ministers in America to support me as long as the Chapel was multiplying in numbers. But this did not happen. People would come to hear me and notice more empty seats than were filled. One president of a prominent Bible college came with an invitation in his pocket to invite me to be the commencement speaker at his college, but when he saw how few there were, he did not even come back to greet me.

But there is a silver lining in all this. I found my true friends. I knew that *pride* was at the bottom of this opposition and diminishing of friendships. Those who once saw me as the wave of the future now felt safe in criticising me. They concluded I would not be a success at Westminster, that I wasn't going to make it. They thought I would be resigning almost any day, that I would not return to London after our summer vacation. Places where I had usually preached in America were also closing down to me. I knew it was because I was no longer seen as a great success. It did not help the ministers' reputation to be closely associated with me anymore. It hurt a lot – that is, it hurt my pride. But it made me see who my true friends were.

There was another fringe benefit. I speak now of a friendship with Jesus. A true friend indeed. He became more real to me than I had known since 1955. Insights into Scripture began to flow. Those truths I had discovered up to then began to be more refined. Psalm 25:14 comes to mind. There are three translations of this verse, all of which I love. First, 'The secret of the Lord is with them that fear him' (KJV). God shares secrets with us. This means there are some things we don't tell to anybody. I sometimes think God would share more with us if we could keep quiet about it. Joseph's folly was telling his dreams to his brothers (Genesis 37:5–9). It's our pride that makes us want to share the Lord's secrets – the worst form of name-dropping. 'The Lord confides in those who fear him' (NIV). This too suggests that we don't tell some things He reveals to us. He shares His deep secrets with those He trusts. 'The friendship of the Lord is for those who fear him' (ESV). There were two people in the Bible – besides the disciples – called God's friend: Abraham (2 Chronicles 20:7; Isaiah 41:8; James 2:23) and Moses: 'The Lord would speak to Moses face to face, as a man speaks with his friend' (Exodus 33:11). Jesus said to his disciples, '"I have called you friends, for everything that I learned from my Father I have made known to you"' (John 15:15). It is a wonderful, wonderful privilege to be God's friend.

Whereas we certainly have a right to choose our friends, the truth is that God chooses them for us. His idea of who would be a good and faithful friend is better than anything we could have come up with. But as I said above, there are levels of friends. I have had those who claimed to be my friend, only to find that they were not true friends after all. There were even those who tried to get close to me – and be seen as my friend – because they thought I would fail at the Chapel and they wanted to be at the top of the queue among those who might qualify as my successor.

You need friends who will not be ashamed of what you believe or those who are already your friends. Paul said to Timothy that he should not be ashamed of the gospel 'or ashamed of me his prisoner' (2 Timothy 1:8). There is not a lot that a prisoner can do for you! And Paul wasn't coming out of prison either! And yet he asked that Timothy be not ashamed of him. Would you have been ashamed to be Paul's friend? You would almost certainly say that you would be honoured to be such. Yes. But in those days Paul was not seen as a valuable person to know. He was only barely accepted by the disciples of Jesus. His view of justification by faith went into details that none of the original followers of Jesus would have fathomed. They accepted him in the end – but only just.

The late T. W. Wilson used to write to me once in a while. He was Billy Graham's closest friend. He honoured me by having me sit with him once (right behind Billy) at a Billy Graham meeting in Wembley stadium. Although I was not really close to T. W. (Billy called him 'T'), he always signed a letter to me 'Your true friend'. I always felt he meant that. A true friend does not have to be a close friend. Funnily enough a close friend may not be a true friend. But I want to be a true friend – to everybody.

I thank God for my friends. As Larry King said last night as he was going off the air, 'Money can't buy friends'. But the kind of friends you want at the end of the day are those who rejoice in what you rejoice in – that they love the Gospel supremely and are carefully obedient to the Holy Spirit. With that combination and with those qualifications you get the greatest fringe benefit of all: God as your true and best friend. It doesn't get better than that.

12

HOW TO BECOME YESTERDAY'S MAN

'The Lord said to Samuel, "How long will you mourn for Saul, since I have rejected him as king over Israel? Fill your horn with oil and be on your way; I am sending you to Jesse of Bethlehem. I have chosen one of his sons to be king."'

I Samuel 16:1

'It is impossible for those who have once been enlightened, who have tasted the heavenly gift, who have shared in the Holy Spirit, who have tasted the goodness of the word of God and the powers of the coming age, if they fall away, to be brought back to repentance, because to their loss they are crucifying the Son of God all over again and subjecting him to public disgrace.'

Hebrews 6:4–6

'There are no exceptions to the rule that everybody likes to be an exception to the rule.'

Charles Osgood

'The worst thing that can happen to a man is to succeed before he is ready.'

D. M. Lloyd-Jones (1899–1981)

Nobody wants to be yesterday's man or woman. We all want to feel needed, to be wanted and to be in demand to some extent. Here I am, seventy-five years old, and maintaining a lifestyle as if I were thirty-five. I am so blessed, and I am so grateful. I do not deserve this. I have given God good reason to take His hand off me many times over the years by grieving the Holy Spirit. But He has been gracious to me. There is no explanation but His sheer mercy. A few years ago Billy Graham expressed his greatest fear, 'that God would take His hand off me'. Billy knew the true explanation for his success: God's hand on him.

In Chapter 6, *When the Anointing Lifts*, we saw what can happen to the person who grieves the Holy Spirit and who is left to themselves – and how pride sets in. But the lifting of the anointing can be temporary. I can testify to this. It need not be permanent. For when we grieve the Holy Spirit and realise it, we can repent and be restored.

The meaning of Hebrews 6:4–6

And yet Hebrews 6:4–6 describes those who fall away and cannot be renewed again to repentance. Whatever does this mean? You may recall that I stated in Chapter 10 that I had a major change regarding the meaning of this passage. It did not constitute a theological change but only how this passage applies to Christians. It came in 1982 while we were in the midst of a series on Hebrews. Whereas I had for over twenty years taken a common reformed view that those described in this passage were counterfeit believers, I became convinced that these verses describe those truly converted. For one thing I reasoned: if the writer did want to describe *saved* people, how else could he describe them but that they were enlightened, had tasted of Jesus Christ, tasted the goodness of God's word and who shared – 'were made partakers of' (KJV) – the Holy Spirit? I upheld a view that was safeguarding certain reformed presuppositions more than it was the truth. Regarding the word 'tasted', some argue that you can taste without swallowing. So I asked, what did it mean that Jesus 'tasted death' (Hebrews 2:9)? The truth is, these are converted people described in Hebrews 6:4–6 who had become stone deaf to the Spirit.

This passage has been a theological battleground between Calvinists and Arminians for years. Calvinists claim a Christian cannot fall away; this passage says one can indeed fall away. In fact the Greek word is a passive participle – 'having fallen away' – which suggests some were already in that state. There is not 'if' in the Greek, although it may well be implied. Arminians claim you can fall away but they equally and adamantly teach that if you do fall you can be restored; this passage says you cannot be. '... it is impossible, in the case of those who have once been enlightened ... and then have fallen away, to restore them again to repentance ...' (ESV).

Key verse: Hebrews 5:11

The key verse is Hebrews 5:11, that describes these Hebrew Christians as already being 'dull of hearing' (KJV, ESV). In other words, they were hard of hearing, spiritually speaking, and were in danger of reaching the juncture they would be completely deaf – and not hear God speak at all. '"Today, if you hear his voice"', God said to his ancient people in the desert (Hebrews 3:7 quoting Psalm 95:7). As long as we can hear God's voice, we are not stone deaf to the Spirit – praise the Lord! But those who did not listen to God's voice reached the place where '... it is impossible ... to renew them *again* unto repentance' (Hebrews 6:4, 6 KJV), or 'to be *brought back* to repentance' (NIV), which shows they had been granted repentance at some point in their lives – which proves they had been saved. Such people, then, could not be renewed to repentance again. Their privilege of being renewed was over. To be renewed means to be changed from 'glory to glory' (2 Corinthians 3:18 KJV). To become stone deaf to the Spirit means there is no possibility of being renewed because these people can no longer hear God speak – ever. Their fall, then, was not from a state of being saved but (1) from the state of being *renewed so they could hear God speak* and (2) from any reward at the Judgment Seat of Christ.

I believe I have met Christians like this. Although I can't say this for sure – I am not their judge – one can nonetheless see fairly obvious indications that such people knew the Lord but did not take the manifest presence of the Holy Spirit seriously. Ananias and Sapphira, seen above, are examples of this.

King Saul

This is what happened to King Saul. He was not only sought after and found by Samuel (1 Samuel 9), then converted (1 Samuel 10:9) but was given prophetic powers (1 Samuel 10:6, 10–12). He is a perfect example of those described in Hebrews 6:4–6. The 'falling away' should not be seen as merely a moral failure. David had a moral failure and was restored (2 Samuel 11–12; Psalm 51). The falling away in Hebrews 6:4–6 refers to those who deliberately and consciously ignore an explicit scriptural principle, cross over a line and then become yesterday's men and women. It need not happen to you or me. But it could.

By 'yesterday's men or women', I refer to the fact that in former years such people were truly being used of God, possibly right in the middle of what God was doing – but only in the past. No longer. So I call them 'yesterday's' men or women because they are irrelevant today. It does not mean they are old or retired. It does not mean they have been made redundant. As a matter of fact they could be active in their church and in ministry. As someone put it regarding the church, 'If the Holy Spirit were completely taken from the church today, 90 per cent of the work of the church would go right on as if nothing happened', this can happen to an individual – as described in Hebrews 6:4–6. You can be old and be tomorrow's man; you can be young and can be yesterday's man or woman. Moses was eighty before he was truly used of God; King Saul was only forty when he became yesterday's man. It has to do with crossing over a line that so offends the Holy Spirit, His voice is never again perceived in one's heart.

But there is a frightful irony here: because the gifts and calling of God are 'irrevocable' (Romans 11:29), their gift could flourish – as if nothing had happened. King Saul prophesied immediately after his conversion; he continued to prophesy after he became yesterday's man! Indeed, strange as this may seem, on his way to kill young David he 'prophesied' (1 Samuel 19:23–24). This explains how well-known TV evangelists' gifts flourished simultaneously with their double lifestyle. Not all are struck dead like Ananias and Sapphira. Indeed, King Saul lived another twenty years. But he never amounted to anything that was honouring to God – ever. He spent the whole of his kingship trying to get rid of David.

The steps toward becoming yesterday's man

We can learn from Saul. As he became yesterday's man, we can look at his life and learn how *not* to be if we do not want to become yesterday's man or woman.

First, he would not accept the limits of his calling. He was called to be a king, not a priest. But he decided to do the duty of a priest – on his own. Here is what happened: he was instructed by Samuel to wait until Samuel showed up. But Samuel was running late. King Saul became impatient and stepped in to do what he was never called to do: '"Bring me the burnt offering and fellowship offerings"' (1 Samuel 13:8–9).

You and I have a limit to our gifting, calling or anointing. We have a 'measure' of faith (Romans 12:3). This means there is a limit to our gift, or calling. But King Saul wasn't prepared to accept any limits on his calling. You would have thought that being king was enough! But no. 'Bring me the burnt offering.' He crossed over a line – and knew exactly what he was doing. It was as though he said, 'I'm king, aren't I? I can do whatever I choose to do'.

You and I may not feel that our limit – or measure – of faith is very great. This may cause us to be a bit envious of one who has a greater measure of faith. But God takes the responsibility for our lot in life. We must accept what he gives and not look over our shoulder – and covet another person's calling or gifting. 'Do not think of yourself more highly than you ought, but rather think of yourself with sober judgment, in accordance with the *measure of faith* God has given you' (Romans 12:3). Be content with the way God has made you and prepared you:

> There is some place for you to fill, some work for you to do
> That no one can or ever will do quite as well as you.
> It may lie close along your way – some homely little duty
> That only needs your touch, your sway to blossom into beauty.

Anonymous

Second, he took himself too seriously. It was *pride* at the bottom of his fatal decision to offer the burnt offering. He showed contempt for Samuel – the legendary prophet who was deeply admired by the people. This was Saul's chance to upstage Samuel.

The surest way to become yesterday's man

Third, he put himself above the word of God. This was the most serious issue of all. Exodus, Leviticus, Numbers and Deuteronomy indicate that only the person called of God could be a priest and offer sacrifices. Saul decided he wanted to be a priest for a few moments. He wasn't content with being king!

I would lovingly say to you, dear reader, that the quickest and surest way to become yesterday's man or woman is for you and me to put ourselves above the word of God. You may say, 'Others should have to adhere to Scripture, yes, but I am the exception to the rule'. That is what all fallen Christian leaders assumed, that they were the exception to the rule. Wrong. Nobody – ever – should do anything so foolish as to think you can by-pass Holy Scripture. We are all to be under the word of God. We are subservient to it. We must all obey it. 'I the Lord do not change' (Malachi 3:6).

Fourth, he let the unexpected circumstances dictate the way forward in the immediate situation. He said to Samuel, '"... I saw that the men were scattering, and that you did not come at the set time ... I thought, 'Now the Philistines will come down against me at Gilgal, and I have not sought the Lord's favour ...'"' (1 Samuel 13:11–12). This, to Saul, gave him the right to do the work of a priest.

Not accepting the blame

Fifth, he blamed Samuel for the whole thing. '"… you did not come at the set time …"' (1 Samuel 13:11). He passed the buck to Samuel who had agreed to show up in seven days (v. 8), but Samuel did not turn up on time. So Saul took over.

The 'blame game' is an ancient enterprise. It started in the Garden of Eden. Adam blamed Eve. She blamed the serpent (Genesis 3:12–13) How many a fallen Christian leader let a thousand matters give them an excuse to blame someone for their behaviour – their leaders, their wives, their friends.

Sixth, Saul let his feelings – not Scripture – govern his decision to offer the burnt offerings. '"… I felt compelled to offer the burnt offerings"' (1 Samuel 13:12). It is like saying, 'I felt led to do this'. Have you ever heard of someone who said, 'God told me to do this' – when it was right against clear teaching in the Bible?

Any leading of the Holy Spirit must be tested by Scripture

Any 'leading' you and I get in this world will cohere with biblical teaching if it is a word from God. The Bible is the Holy Spirit's greatest product. He wrote it (2 Timothy 3:16; 2 Peter 1:21). To quote Dr Martyn Lloyd-Jones: 'The Bible was not given to replace the miraculous – including hearing God speak to you as he did to Philip in Acts 8:26, 29 – but to correct abuses.' His point is: we always bow to Scripture as the ultimate way God speaks to us; He will never speak in a manner that goes against the written word.

Being accountable

Seventh, King Saul was accountable to nobody. He should have been accountable to Samuel his mentor. But no, he would not listen to Samuel but wanted to argue with him. You and I need to be accountable to people here below. Don't say, 'I am accountable ultimately only to God'. That of course is true. But the proof you are accountable to God – and want to please him – will be that you have *people* here on this earth who will know all about you and hold your feet to the fire.

Here are the famous last words of every fallen Christian leader: 'I am accountable to *God.*' I'm sorry, but that isn't good enough! You need men (if you are a man) or women (if you are a woman) around you to whom you will be answerable. You and I need friends who will severely love us – and not let us get away with anything that could possibly bring an end to our influence.

God actually gave Saul another chance. Read 1 Samuel 15 when Saul was commanded to destroy totally everything that belonged to the Amalekites. '"Do not spare them; put to death men and women, children and infants, cattle and sheep, camels and donkeys"' (1 Samuel 15:3). You and I may not completely understand this, but never forget that God's ways are higher than our ways (Isaiah 55:9). As Abraham put it – a verse Mrs Martyn Lloyd-Jones always hung on to: '"Will not the Judge of all the earth do right?"' (Genesis 18:25).

Saul blew it again. God said to him, '"You have rejected the word of the Lord, and the Lord has rejected you as king over Israel"' (1 Samuel 15:26). Curiously Saul remained king for many more years. He continued on as though Samuel had approved of him.

Saul had such a brilliant beginning. Early on '... the Spirit of God came upon him in power, and he burned with anger. He took a pair of oxen, cut them into pieces, and sent the pieces by messengers throughout Israel, proclaiming, "This is what will be done to the oxen of anyone who does not follow Saul and Samuel." Then the terror of the Lord fell on the people, and they turned out as one man' (1 Samuel 11:6–7). A good beginning does not necessarily mean a good ending.

Symptoms of being yesterday's man

There followed certain symptoms which further show the folly of pride. Saul became consumed with jealousy. After David killed Goliath and the women sang, '"Saul has slain his thousands, and

David his tens of thousands." Saul was very angry; ... from that time on Saul kept a jealous eye on David' (1 Samuel 18:7–9. In fact so gripped by jealousy was King Saul that he feared David more than he did the enemy of Israel – the Philistines!

Saul could not even keep his word to his son Jonathan. Jonathan pleaded with his father to cut David some slack. Saul even swore an oath that he would not lay a finger on David. '"As surely as the Lord lives, David will not be put to death"' (1 Samuel 19:6). There were two things going on here; Saul broke his word to his son, but also even broke the oath he swore to God! Yesterday's man will almost always be characterised by a compromised integrity.

It all began with pride.

13

PROPHETIC PRIDE

'But Jonah was greatly displeased and became angry. He prayed to the Lord, "O Lord, is this not what I said when I was still at home? That is why I was so quick to flee to Tarshish. I knew that you are a gracious and compassionate God, slow to anger and abounding in love, a God who relents from sending calamity. Now, O Lord, take away my life, for it is better for me to die than to live". But the Lord replied, "Have you any right to be angry?"'

Jonah 4:1–4

'Vindicate me, O Lord ...'

Psalm 26:1

'Pride is an admission of weakness; it secretly fears all competition and dreads all rivals.'

Fulton J. Sheen (1895–1979)

'The noble art of losing face may some day save the human race and turn into eternal merit what weaker minds would call disgrace.'

Piet Hein (1905–1996)

Until 1990 I largely thought of 'prophecy' in terms of eschatology – future events that precede the Second Coming of Jesus. When I first started preaching (at the age of nineteen) I thought I knew everything – the infallible meaning of Daniel, Matthew 24 and the book of Revelation. I now would be afraid to claim I understand these passages! But in 1990 my understanding of the word 'prophecy' and 'prophetic' began to shift. While I am more interested than ever in eschatology, I now understand the word prophecy in three ways: (1) what is eschatological, (2) preaching as being prophetic and (3) the gift of prophecy being available in the body of Christ. Unless one is a 'cessationist' – the belief that all things miraculous ceased with the early church, there is no reason to question whether an Elijah, Deborah or Samuel could emerge today – as long as he or she is utterly and totally subservient to Scripture. No matter how awesome one's gift is in this area – or how high their profile might be – the Bible alone is infallible.

This means that a prophetic person needs a lot of humility. They have to admit it when they get it wrong. They are understandably loath to do so. They want to be trusted and believed, and they fear that if they have a prophecy that was not accurate, nobody would believe them any longer. This is why they need a lot of humility – to be able to carry on after a mistake and leave it to God to vindicate their word.

The Kansas City Prophets

In 1990 a book by Bishop David Pytches called *The Kansas City Prophets* caused no small stir in Britain. My own reaction was very negative, but I began to change my mind after I met some of these men. I now know all of those who are featured in the book. My point is this: I widened my perspective with regard to the prophetic. Some of them have done us a lot of good. In recent years I have however become almost disillusioned regarding this new openness to the prophetic – seeing how some of them turned out – but in retrospect I would say it has done far more good than harm.

The big thing I have come to see first-hand is, (1) these men are very human indeed, (2) their gift does not function twenty-four hours a day, (3) they do get it wrong sometimes and (4) they are slow to admit their mistakes. I once asked one of them, 'Have you ever got it wrong?' 'No, I never have', he replied with a straight face. But I know better.

Prophetic people suffer a lot. For one thing, as Paul needed a 'thorn in the flesh' to keep him humble (2 Corinthians 12:7), so too do these people undergo a lot of persecution, sometimes illness and hurt that, probably, is needed lest they take themselves too seriously. One of the problems they face is, (1) the people to whom they give a prophetic word *always* seem to want more – an elaboration on what was spoken – which these people have no time for; (2) their prophecies can take a long time before they are fulfilled – which sometimes causes people openly to question them and bother them all the more; and (3) they are besieged non-stop after services or in hotel lobbies with strangers approaching them , 'Do you have a word for me?' (as if they were almost divine).

Meeting prophetic people has helped me to understand the human nature of the Elijahs or Jonahs of this world. James reminded us that Elijah was 'a man with a nature like ours' (James 5:17 ESV). We also saw in this book how Elijah took himself too seriously, claiming that he was the only true prophet left – but he was so wrong!

Jonah

I chose the book of Jonah as my first series of sermons at Westminster Chapel. People asked me why I chose Jonah. It was largely because I am a Jonah. I so identify with him – whether the Jonah on the run from God's voice or the Jonah that was so selfish and proud when he was not vindicated. It is *so* encouraging to discover again and again that God uses imperfect people. That is why the book of Jonah encourages me.

Jonah's chief problem was that he could not think outside the 'Israel box', that is, he could not abide God being nice to any nation but Israel. Israel was God's chosen people and nation. But a good bit of national and racial pride set in. Israelites grew up believing they were 'it' and that all other nations were inferior, deprived, pitiful and hopeless. When God first said to Jonah, '"Go to the great city of Nineveh and preach against it, because its wickedness has come up before me"' (Jonah 1:2), we are not told at first why Jonah said No! and went in the opposite direction. I used to think it was merely because he was afraid of the persecution that would come from this. But that was not the reason he ran: he feared the worst – that God would be merciful to the Ninevites and let them off the hook.

Jonah got on a ship that was going to Tarshish, possibly in Celicia, or in ancient Spain. But God sent a wind so strong that the sailors turned to Jonah to see who he was. He came clean and told them, '"I am a Hebrew"' – adding that the storm would not calm down unless they threw him overboard since he was the cause of the problem (Jonah 1:9, 12). They did, but a big fish swallowed him up (v. 17). For three days in the belly of the fish Jonah prayed to get to do what he had not wanted to do – to have a second chance to obey God. God granted it, the fish ejected Jonah on dry land (Jonah 2) and God renewed the order: '"Go to the great city of Nineveh and proclaim to it the message I give you"' (Jonah 3:2).

Jonah's unconditional prophecy

Here was the message: '"Forty more days and Nineveh will be destroyed"' (Jonah 3:4). That was it. There were no conditions – no 'ifs'. He did not say, "Forty more days and Nineveh will be destroyed *if you don't turn from your sins*". No. It was clear and straightforward: *in forty days God will destroy you.* Jonah *might* have added a face-saving condition: you will be destroyed unless you repent. Had he been allowed to throw in a condition, Jonah would have been in a win-win situation. Either way he would have been vindicated. But Jonah was not allowed to add a word to his prophecy; he had orders to preach '"the message I give you"' (Jonah 3:2). And that is what he gave.

Jonah's greatest fears were realised. He feared *all along*, knowing the character of God as he did, that God would grant repentance to the people of Nineveh. And God did precisely that. 'When God saw what they did and how they turned from their evil ways, he had compassion and did not bring upon them the destruction he had threatened' (Jonah 3:10).

God sent revival. The instrument was Jonah. 'But Jonah was greatly displeased and became angry' (Jonah 4:1). Isn't this amazing? What preacher today would not be thrilled if he were used to bring revival to a great city?

Why was Jonah angry? Two reasons: (1) his racial and national prejudice and (2) his prophetic reputation.

It turns out that Jonah had a conversation with God upon hearing the original command to go to Nineveh: '"... is this not what I said when I was still at home? That is why I was so quick to flee to Tarshish. I knew that you are a gracious and compassionate God, slow to anger and abounding in love, a God who relents from sending calamity"' (Jonah 4:2). The last thing Jonah wanted was for God to be good to a country other than Israel.

Jonah can hardly take credit for his obedience. He had little choice. He was dying and miserable in the belly of the fish. It was as though God put a pistol to his head! As they sang in the hills of Kentucky, 'He doesn't compel us against our will but makes us willing to go'. It will be that way with all of us. None of us can take a single ounce of credit for our obedience. We will not only comply with, but agree with those words of Jesus: '"So you also, when you have done everything you were told to do, should say, 'We are unworthy servants; we have only done our duty'"' (Luke 17:10).

In a word: God got all the glory, Jonah got none.

But there is more: his reputation as a prophet. Because there were no conditions attached to his warning – but only that Nineveh categorically would be destroyed, Jonah is seen as having got it wrong. He cared more for his reputation than the glory of God. Jonah lost face. God is looking for those who will willingly lose face.

There is no limit to how far a person can go, as long as he doesn't care who gets the credit for it. And in the case of the Nineveh revival, although Jonah was the sovereign vessel that brought about the awakening, he got no pleasure in it. He was virtually forced to go to Nineveh and then not allowed to enjoy it. I do remember one of the Kansas City prophets saying to me, 'The more God uses me, the less I am able enjoy it'.

Could you live with that? Could I?

Jonah's three-fold prejudices

Jonah had three prejudices to overcome. First, a theological prejudice. It was God's idea to choose Israel. He grew up believing from his mother's knee that God had a special love for Israel, that this was particular, special and irrevocable. The thought of God doing anything outside Israel was unthinkable. But at the same time Jonah got to know the true God. '"I knew that you are a gracious and compassionate God"' (Jonah 4:2), therefore he feared that this part of God's character might spill over on Nineveh. Secondly, Jonah was filled with national prejudice. He loved Israel. He was patriotic. To march into Nineveh would make him feel disloyal. And if, as he feared, God would be merciful to the Ninevites, how would this make him look before his fellow Israelites? Thirdly, Jonah was racially prejudiced. He was biased toward his own race and felt animosity and superiority toward Gentiles, especially a nation like Assyria of which Nineveh was a part (Mosul in Iraq today). The thought of mixing with them was distasteful to him.

This theological, national and racial prejudice was deeply ingrained in the Jews. It is striking that Paul, addressing Jews in Jerusalem, was being listened to – that is, until he mentioned that God was sending him 'to the *Gentiles*'. Think of this: no one said a word when he mentioned his background (Acts 22:3), his persecuting Christians (vv. 4–5), his extraordinary conversion (vv. 6–10), making his way to Damascus (v. 11), his healing of blindness (v. 13), God's direct word to him (v. 14), his being baptised (v. 16), his direct word from Jesus (v. 18) and his reply (vv. 19–20). So far, so good, It was not until Paul quoted Jesus saying, '"'*Go; I will send you far away to the Gentiles*'"' (v. 21) that pandemonium broke loose. 'The crowd listened to Paul until he said this. Then they raised their voices and shouted, "Rid the earth of him! He's not fit to live!"' (Acts 22:22).

These are the very kind of biases Jonah had. But God used him!

David Brainerd (1718–1747)

When at Oxford I became acquainted with the biographer of David Brainerd, the missionary to the New York Indians in the early eighteenth century. Had Brainerd lived he would have become Jonathan Edwards' son-in-law, but he died at the age of twenty-nine. He is legendary to this day. Edwards published 'The Life and Diary of David Brainerd'. John Wesley urged all Methodist ministers to read it. There was a time when that little book – so inspiring – was once said to have put more people on the mission field than any piece of literature other than the Bible. But here is the irony: David Brainerd did not like the Indians to whom he ministered! His biographer actually said to me, 'He hated them'. Whether this was literally true or not, God used him powerfully.

I don't think the Apostle Paul was too happy when he was told he must be a minister to the Gentiles. Every Jew grew up with a prejudice against those outside their 'box'. Paul *so* wanted to reach his own people. He had the credentials (see Philippians 3:5–6). His teacher was the famed Gamaliel (Acts 22:3). But No, said God, it will be Gentiles for you, Paul (Galatians 2:9). Paul still did all he could to reach Jews (see Romans 9:1ff.) That was the real reason he insisted on going to Jerusalem all along, to which I referred above.

I did give a prophecy to the Wembley Conference Centre in London in 1992. It got me into more trouble than any sermon I ever preached. In it I said that a move of the Holy Spirit much, much greater than the Charismatic Movement is coming – I called it 'Isaac'. I hold that as Abraham sincerely thought that Ishmael was the child that had been promised to him, so many Charismatics believe that they represent the long awaited movement of the Spirit prior to the Second Coming. But they are 'Ishmael' – for whom great things were nonetheless promised. 'Isaac' is coming, however, although it did not please Abraham at first (Genesis 17:18). This message did not please many Charismatics at first either. But I maintain that as the promise regarding Isaac was a hundred times greater than that pertaining to Ishmael, so we will see in similar proportion an unprecedented movement of the Spirit coming down the road that exceeds all this planet has ever witnessed. It will transcend all theological, geographical, racial, cultural and ecclesiastical lines. It is when the Word and Spirit simultaneously come together – at last. I can indeed therefore understand prophetic pride; I would love that prophecy to be vindicated.

Smith Wigglesworth (1859–1947)

However, forty-five years before my own statement above, there came a word from Smith Wigglesworth who, during the year he died, reportedly made this statement: 'During the next few decades there will be two distinct moves of the Holy Spirit across the Church in Great Britain. The first move will affect every Church that is open to receive it and will be characterised by a restoration of the baptism and gifts of the Holy Spirit. The second move of the Holy Spirit will result in people leaving historic Churches and planting new Churches. In the duration of each of these moves, the people who are involved will say, "This is the great revival". But the Lord says "No, neither is the great revival but both are steps towards it". When the new Church phase is on the wane, there will be evidenced in the Churches something that has not been seen before: a coming together of those with an emphasis on the Word and those with the emphasis on the Spirit. When the Word and the Spirit come together, there will be the biggest movement of the Holy Spirit that the nation, and indeed the world, have ever seen. It will mark the beginning of a revival that will eclipse anything that has been witnessed within these shores, even the Wesleyan and the Welsh revivals of former years. The outpouring of God's Spirit will flow over from the United Kingdom to the mainland of Europe and, from there, will begin a missionary move to the ends of the earth.'

That too is a word that is as yet unfulfilled. But here is what you can count on. When the great movement of the Holy Spirit comes, whatever nickname may be attached to it, God will get all the glory – and all of us who are Jonahs will have to stand aside. In the case of Jonah, to his credit when telling his story, he gave God the last word (see Jonah 4:11).

14

HYPOCRITICAL HUMILITY

'He [Herod] sent them [the Magi] to Bethlehem and said, "Go and make a careful search for the child. As soon as you find him, report to me, so that I too may go and worship him."'

Matthew 2:8

'"Teacher", they said, "we know you are a man of integrity and that you teach the way of God in accordance with the truth. You aren't swayed by men, because you pay no attention to who they are."'

Matthew 22:16

'Be modest! It is the kind of pride least likely to offend.'

Jules Renard (1864–1910)

'I have also known some men appear very humble just to gain their own ends; and when an unrenewed man puts on humility merely as a cloak, I was going to say that he is devilish, for the very humble man who aims at making some gain by it – the Uriah Heep of the novelist – is one of the most despicable of all people beneath the sky.'

Charles H. Spurgeon (1834–1892)

In Chapter 10 I referred to 'eating humble pie'. The origin of this expression is apparently traced to 'numbles' – a name given to a deer's entrails. The name eventually became 'umbles' and these were used as an ingredient in pies. The fact that umble pie was often eaten by those of a humble situation is possibly the reason that 'eating humble pie' gained its idiomatic meaning. Uriah Heep, the fictional character created by Charles Dickens (1812–1870), became notorious as calling himself a 'very *'umble* man'. There are people who still pronounce humble has ''umble'. Some seem to think it is an act of humility actually to say ''umble' rather than 'humble'! I will never forget being put in my place when I referred to someone as humble. 'You should say *'umble*', a man patronisingly scolded me. The Uriah Heeps of this world are alive and well!

Since humility is an obvious virtue and admired by most people, many try to feign humility. It looks better if you appear humble. As for those who are proud of their humility, this of course is an impossibility – it is like trying to make a hot snowball! And yet people try to play the role of being humble, don't they?

There are of course those who don't try to show humility – and probably get away with it. The architect Frank Lloyd Wright (1867–1959) said, 'Early in life I had to choose between honest arrogance and hypocritical humility. I chose the former and have seen no reason to change'. When Jack Benny said, 'Modesty is my best quality', he was joking of course; his forte was always deprecating himself – which endeared him to the public.

Appearing to be modest is the safest kind of pride. You hope that most people won't see through you. You must not look too much like Uriah Heep – or you will blow your cover. One learns how to speak modestly, gratefully and sincerely. If preaching is an art, so is feigning modesty. Practice make perfect. The prouder you are, the better you probably get at it – certainly with a little experience! Body language too can have a lot to do it. Although you must stand erect, keeping your head slightly bowed or tilted with a slightly surprised but unworthy look on your face, often goes down fairly well – especially with those who resent any hint of assertiveness or confidence. With practice you can look very impressive indeed. And when you receive a compliment, be sure to frown a tiny bit in order to look humbled or embarrassed. You must by all means conceal that you expected the accolade; and do please hide how elated inwardly you actually are.

I grew up in a church that had a rather distorted view of what being humble was. For years the preachers wore black (or very dark suits), the ladies wore modest, colourless clothes with their hair in a bun. It was one of the ways they had of showing how humble they were. This spilt over into strict standards that make one laugh today.

I wore a Geneva gown during my first five years at Westminster. The rationale for this was that it 'covered the man' – this being a sign of humility. Funnily enough, it gave me a feeling of importance; it enhanced my self-esteem in those days. It did not take humility for me to wear that black robe; if anything, it took a bit of humility to give it up – and appear in a dark suit. I was criticised by a few good people for abandoning the robe. And when I wore a grey suit one Sunday morning I was rebuked by a sweet saintly old lady who was okay about the robe but was unhappy that my suit wasn't black. You can't win!

And yet I remember a stringent, old-fashioned minister who wore white! He was Dr E. E. Shelhamer (1869–1940), a Wesleyan Methodist minister who preached against eating pork and hot biscuits among other things. Eating biscuits *cold* apparently showed more humility. I actually saw this man once. I was only five years old – but I remember it to this day. Dr Shelhamer was a legend in the holiness movement – certainly then and perhaps now to some. My dad pointed him out to me at the God's Bible School annual camp meeting in Cincinnati, Ohio. 'There he is, my son', I can remember my dad saying, almost in a whisper. Shelhamer was regarded as one of the greatest preachers ever to grace the pulpit. I will never forget seeing him. He was famous for his preaching power and ability, godliness and humility. Here I was only five years old but even I could see, as it were, 'the emperor has no clothes'! I couldn't get away from the fact that this godly, humble man wore a brilliantly white suit! It stood out. Nobody else wore a white suit – only E. E. Shelhamer. No one else *dare* wear a white suit. I think he might have resented it if another person wore a white suit with him around. But with his rather long white hair in that snow white suit it was an impressive sight indeed. If one did not know who he was, I think they may well have asked! You could not help but notice him. Looking back I can see it was as if he was wearing a costume. He had to know he stood out in the crowd. And yet it did not seem to occur to anyone that this man was as proud as a peacock. Or as Johann Wolfgang von Goethe (1749–1832) put it, 'Too rigid scruples are concealed pride'.

I reckon the Pharisees who sent their disciples to trap Jesus coached them in appearing humble and sincere. They needed all the help they could get. When we get to heaven we can ask for a DVD of that occasion when they said to Jesus, 'We know you are a man of integrity, you teach the truth, you aren't swayed by men, nor do you pay any attention to who they are'. Assuming their body language and facial expressions seemed sufficiently sincere and pious, most of us would have fallen for that line like a ton of bricks. But Jesus saw right through them, '"You hypocrites, why are you trying to trap me?"' (Matthew 22:18).

I have learned to be wary of people who pray with a certain pious tone and always use hackneyed language of Zion. But I have done this too. All that I have spoken against and in this book is aimed at me – believe me; in some ways I feel like a fraud in writing this book. But I think it is needed, and who is sufficient for these things? I can only express my concerns, fears, observations and hope that in the process you and I will – however slowly – make progress in eschewing pride and becoming a little more "*umble*"!

A sweet old man – who seemed extremely modest and unpretentious – used to attend our Sunday evening prayer meetings prior to the evening service. His prayers were always edifying, even when he would utter the words 'blessed Jesus' from time to time when there were moments of silence. But one evening, during a communion service, he stood and began speaking in tongues. This had not happened before. A few seconds after he finished (it lasted about thirty seconds) he gave an interpretation. It was fine. Nobody was offended. In fact it was rather sweet. But he did it the following communion service – same thing and the interpretation was the same: 'Thus saith the Lord, I am with thee' – kind benedictory words. It happened the third time – and the fourth: always the same interpretation. By this time, people were dreading the communion services. I finally got the courage to speak to this man. I gently explained that his speaking in tongues and his predictable interpretations were beginning to cause a little unrest. He always seemed so humble and I honestly thought he would meekly appreciate and accept my suggestion that he not do this for a while. To my surprise he was greatly offended, raised his voice and became very defensive. I have never seen him since. I felt bad about it. I had hoped he was *truly* a humble man. 'Swallowing your pride seldom leads to indigestion', said Benedict de Spinoza (1632–1677), but this man sadly could not do that.

Many years ago – when nearly everybody used only the King James Version – there came a song that was almost like a protest against Jesus' words: '"In my Father's house are many mansions: if it were not so, I would have told you. I go to prepare a place for you"' (John 14:2 KJV). Most versions today translate the Greek word *monee* as 'rooms' rather than 'mansions'. In any case, we all assumed that when we get to heaven we will live in a magnificent mansion. We speculated how high, how wide, how fancy, how big. But then came a song – no one seems to know who wrote it – called 'Lord build me just a *cabin* in the corner of glory land'. If this isn't a 'Uriah Heep' song, I don't know what is. The idea is this: I don't need a big mansion up in heaven – I'm not worthy of a mansion, just a little cabin will do. By 'cabin' they mean a simple, small and plain one-room log cabin that they were happy with in the hills of Kentucky.

> Many years I've been lookin' for a place to call home
> But I've failed here to find it so I must travel on;
> I don't care for fine mansions on earth's sinkin' sand;
> Lord build me a cabin in the corner of glory land.
> Lord build me just a cabin in the corner of glory land;
> In the shade of the tree of life that it may ever stand;
> Where I can just hear the angels sing and shake Jesus' hand;
> Lord, build me a cabin in the corner of glory land.
>
> Anonymous

The next verse includes the lines 'I know I'm not worthy of such splendour', but 'I'm asking for mercy while I humbly stand'. In Hank Williams' recording, he sings "*umbly*". The song states basically three things: (1) I'm not worthy of a mansion ; Lord build me just a cabin; (2) I don't expect to be right in the centre of heaven, only in a 'corner of glory land'; and (3) I don't anticipate getting to spend time with Jesus – little ole' me – but only to shake his hand!

There seems to be a need all over the world to appear humble – whether in how low you bow in the Orient or how imperceptibly you dress down amongst gentry in England. When American tourists come to Britain in their flashy clothes they have no idea how they are perceived but are amazed at how simply the upper class Brit dresses. When we lived in London, our neighbour was a former principal of an Oxford college and member of the House of Lords. He would sit on a bench outside our flat and, if you didn't already know, you might mistake him for a beggar! There is in middle class Britain a disdain for being 'assertive' – to stand out. There is safety in appearing modest.

And yet sometimes hiding what you really are is not so subtle. When King Herod got word that kings from the east were searching for the newly born king of the Jews, he was deeply threatened. He panicked and sent for the Magi to get more details. Feigning humility, concern and honour for this child he ordered them to carry on to find him. '"As soon as you find him, report to me, so that I too may go and worship him"' (Matthew 2:8).

One of the ways Absalom stole the hearts of the people was by feigning a concern for the people's needs. '"If only I were appointed judge in the land! Then everyone who has a complaint or case could come to me and I would see that he receives justice"'. Also, whenever anyone approached him to bow down before him, Absalom would reach out his hand, take hold of him and kiss him. Absalom behaved in this way towards all the Israelites who came to the king asking for justice, and so he stole the hearts of the men of Israel' (2 Samuel 15:1–6).

The truth is, we are all proud men and women. We may pretend to be rid of it. But if we push it down into the cellar it comes out in the attic. We may succeed for a while in making others think we are not so proud, but God knows the truth. I see the only way forward as looking straight to Jesus – and nowhere else. Charles Spurgeon once said, 'I looked to Christ and the Dove flew in; I looked to the Dove and he disappeared'. That is the way it is with trying to be humble. Do not try so hard, just look to Jesus.

15

BOASTING

'Even if I should choose to boast, I would not be a fool, because I would be speaking the truth. But I refrain, so no-one will think more of me than is warranted by what I do or say.'
2 Corinthians 12:6

'Let another praise you, and not your own mouth; someone else, and not your own lips.'
Proverbs 27:2

'When boasting ends, there dignity begins.'
Owen D. Young (1874–1962)

'The greatest freedom is having nothing to prove.'
Pete Cantrell

I would have thought that boasting is one of the most obvious, unsubtle, counter-productive and unwise things a person could ever do. But we all do it – one way or the other – to some degree. There is more than one definition of boasting. It may be speaking of yourself in superlatives, talking in a self-admiring way or name dropping. In a word: self-praise. Generally speaking, boasting or bragging on oneself does little for the person who hears it.

The antidote to boasting: love – the *agape* love of 1 Corinthians 13:4; for this love 'does not boast'.

Does it bless you when a person continually boasts of who they know, how much time they have spent with famous people and how close they are to them? It feeds on their insatiable ego but does nothing for you! Learn from this; be conscious that when you are boasting of any success, it is probably doing more for you than for them. And what it does for you may well be counter-productive regarding your spiritual life.

Loneliness

However, when it is a *true* friend you are talking with, boasting can be a mutual blessing. We saw above that a true friend is someone who rejoices with you – so too when it comes to boasting: a true friend will enjoy hearing good things that have happened to you. What makes loneliness so awful is that the person cannot share good things – lest the other person plummet or become jealous. Mother Theresa says the greatest problem in the world is loneliness. When Billy Graham preached at Westminster Chapel in 1984 he delivered an unforgettable message on loneliness. So if you have a friend you can boast to, you have a lot to be thankful for.

But the quickest way to put another person off, speaking generally, is to boast. People do not want to hear of your successes; they want to hear about your failures. You can talk about your failures and disappointments to almost anybody; you can only discuss your successes with a true friend.

2 Corinthians 12:6

Once in a great while a verse will leap out at you in a way that makes you see it as though for the first time. In my case, one of those is 2 Corinthians 12:6, a word that I found stunning, transforming and yet extremely difficult to follow through with over the years. For in this verse Paul basically says two things: (1) that he could boast a lot and it all be true, but (2) he refrained from doing it because he would cross over a line and encourage another to think more highly of him than would be pleasing to God. This verse is profound and has been life-changing for me, although I consistently fail to follow it every day as I should. As a matter of fact, it is one of those verses that I read almost every day in order to keep this principle before me. When I preached through 2 Corinthians at Westminster Chapel, it was this verse that meant more to me personally than any other in that series.

Why do we boast? Dale Carnegie says that the greatest urge in humankind is the desire to feel important. Boasting arises from this desire: we hope that others hearing about our accomplishments will give us a feeling of self-importance. In 2 Corinthians 11, Paul took a calculated risk. He decided to boast – but in a surprising manner: to boast of his weaknesses. This culminates in his admitting to an incident for which he had a hard time forgiving himself – when he let people protect him from being hurt as opposed to seeing what God might have done had he not been lowered in a basket from a window (v. 33). At that point he boasts of a 'man in Christ' – as though it were someone else but which is obviously Paul himself – regarding visions and revelations from the Lord (2 Corinthians 12:1–2). He then reaches 2 Corinthians 12:6 in which he says he is governed by a principle that forbids his boasting, 'so no-one will think more of me than is warranted'.

Paul had come to the place that he didn't care what people thought of him. He did of course care; he wanted the Corinthians to know how he loved them and feared their being seduced by enemies of the Gospel. But at the end of the day, Paul watched his words in a manner that would not allow people to think any more of him than what is *warranted*. This meant that Paul had this conviction: God would determine how people thought of him. What was warranted – authorised – was God deciding how highly Paul should be esteemed by people. Paul respected this to the hilt and did not want to cross over a line and violate this principle. The way he spoke therefore was that he restrained himself from saying the slightest thing that would cause people to think more highly of him than God authorised. Like a bridle that controls a horse, then, Paul lived within certain constraints so that people would not admire him one whit more than God had already set for him.

This thought put me to shame. I have sought, ever since I was struck by this verse, to live this way. But I have failed again and again to do so. It is setting an extremely high standard to live by. Even as I write, I am aware that I could be allowing one to admire me more. So I am on a knife-edge; I want to convey the truth as clearly as I can without allowing anybody to have an opinion of me that would dishonour God. If, for example, I told how much I pray every day, could I be boasting – or would my motive be to encourage people everywhere, especially ministers, to pray more? Do I boast by telling you how this verse has gripped me, or would it, by speaking as I do, motivate you to live more like this? That is the delicate balance one seeks to maintain.

And yet I do know how much I have been blessed by another's recounting their successes and failures. Arthur Blessitt, the man who has carried a cross all over the world, has been a tremendous blessing to me. As I have said before, the decision to have him at Westminster Chapel was the best decision I made there in twenty-five years. I would plead with him to share stories. It forced him to boast. But by knowing of certain things, it drew me closer to God! His example on Sunset Strip in Hollywood – witnessing on the streets – became the model for our Pilot Lights. I wouldn't take anything for the things Arthur shared. But some would obviously call it boasting.

My duty therefore is this: to be guarded in all I say lest I cross over a line and encourage one to think of me beyond what God has regarded as the outer limit of admiration.

John 5:44

Here is the key – the verse that transcends all others in this connection: '"How can you believe if you accept praise from one another, yet make no effort to obtain the praise that comes from the only God?"' In this question Jesus unveils the very reason that the Jews missed their promised Messiah. They lived for praise. All they did was done for people to see and admire (Matthew 23:5–7). The idea of receiving the praise from God alone was not on their radar screen. It did not cross their minds to live their lives – and watch their words – so that they might obtain His praise. They *made 'no effort'* to do this, Jesus said. Therefore He asked, 'How *can* you believe?' Surprise, surprise – you *can't* because you are obsessed with the praise of people.

Jonathan Edwards taught us that the task of every generation is to discover in which direction the Sovereign Redeemer is moving, then move in that direction. We would not have a clue in which direction the Holy Spirit might be moving if we did not make every effort to receive the praise that comes from Him.

In the Authorised Version it reads, '"the honour that comes from God only"' – implying that one should want *only* His praise. This should be our aim. If we make every effort to want only His praise – and you get praise from people in the package (without seeking it), God is perhaps okay about that since their praise was not your aim. But our goal, motive, ardent wish, daily desire and fervent prayer should be that we would seek only His praise and honour.

Nothing succeeds like success

One has to take so much boasting among TV preachers with a grain of salt. When it comes to the claim of healing and miracles, for example, one honestly does not know what to believe. The big splash of the so called revival in Lakeland, Florida a few years ago turned out to be virtually nothing. The stories of the miraculous were countless. I accept that a few of them were true because the gifts are irrevocable (Romans 11:29) and God also honours people's sincere faith. In those days friends wrote and telephoned from Britain about the great revival that had broken out in Lakeland. They knew about it before I did. On live television they brought in a man who is famous for his prophetic gift. He said it fulfilled his vision of stadia being filled – that 'this was it', that is the 'last days ministries' which we have all been waiting for. I doubted it from the start and stood largely alone in my claim this whole thing was not of God. I could not imagine that God would be behind such boasting of the evangelist night after night after night. The last claim I heard from them before the meeting closed down was that thirty-seven people were raised from the dead! My reply: if only *one* person were truly raised from the dead (after a death certificate had been issued – which never happened) it would have made the front page of the *New York Times*.

It is the 'hype' one has to wade through. 'Hype' is exaggerated publicity using a questionable claim to intensify the effect in a misleading manner. In order to get people to send in their money, the TV preacher has to make the listener feel they are contributing toward a successful ministry. One hears reports of healings, miracles and blessing. Nothing succeeds like success so these men go on and on in order to get more money. It is all so worldly – 'boasting of what he has and does' (1 John 2:16). The sad thing is, while most people are afraid to criticise what might be of the Holy Spirit, others do not bother to inquire. It has been estimated that 90 per cent of the American population never investigate what they hear on television or read in news papers – they just believe it all.

The greatest freedom of all

It is wicked to play into people's sincere desire to please God by boasting of what cannot be substantiated. And yet the irony is, if the claims *were* true, one would not need to mention them at all! As my friend Pete Cantrell says, 'The greatest freedom is having nothing to prove'. When something is true, you don't need either hype or boasting; you don't even need to say a word!

'When boasting ends, there dignity begins.' The need to boast stems from the need to feel important as well as to get a following. But God has promised to give us all the affirmation we need. If we get *His* praise, what others think is so shallow and unfulfilling. We show ourselves to be truly people of dignity if we say *nothing* that will try to impress another. When I try to impress you, I lost a measure of dignity in that moment as well as forfeiting the praise that would have come from God.

The highest joy imaginable will come on that Day when we hear from the lips of Jesus himself, 'Well done. Good.' I pray that we will somehow wait for that day and not take so seriously what people think of us. What they think of us won't matter then.

16

JUDGING AND BEING JUDGED

'"Do not judge, and you will not be judged. Do not condemn, and you will not be condemned. Forgive, and you will be forgiven. Give, and it will be given to you."'

Luke 6:37

'"If you do away with the yoke of oppression, with the pointing finger and malicious talk ... then your light will rise in the darkness, and your night will become like the noonday."'

Isaiah 58:9–10

'I care very little if I am judged by you or by any human court; indeed, I do not even judge myself. My conscience is clear, but that does not make me innocent. It is the Lord who judges me. Therefore judge nothing before the appointed time; wait till the Lord comes. He will bring to light what is hidden in darkness and will expose the motives of men's hearts. At that time each will receive his praise from God.'

1 Corinthians 4:3–5

'If you judge people, you have no time to love them.'

Mother Theresa (1910–1997)

'I am more afraid of my own heart than of the pope and all his cardinals. I have within me the great pope, Self.'

Martin Luther (1483–1546)

If our boasting puts off others, how much more judging them! And yet both boasting and judging have in common that they originate in pride.

In the previous chapter I mentioned that there are certain verses I read every day. I do this to keep them before me so that, just maybe, I will live according to a certain standard each day. Another of these verses is Luke 6:37: '"Do not judge, and you will not be judged. Do no condemn, and you will not be condemned. Forgive, and you will be forgiven."' You may also recall that I mentioned my old friend Jack Brothers who was a member of Alcoholics Anonymous, that Jack regarded himself as an alcoholic even though he had not tasted alcohol in eleven years. Until the day he died, Jack always prayed at the beginning of each day, 'Get me through this day without a drink'.

When it comes to judging and pointing the finger, I live from day to day. Judging people is possibly my greatest weakness. It stems from pride. And it always grieves the Holy Spirit.

Pride makes us feel worthy to judge another. We think we have made personal progress in a particular area and forget (1) how recently we were like that and (2) how easily we could fall right back into the same malady. Pride is what makes us presume, even if unconsciously, that we are a cut above the other person. The truth is, we are not. Jesus followed his admonition about judging with this question: '"Why do you look at the speck of sawdust in your brother's eye and pay no attention to the plank in your own eye? ... You hypocrite, first take the plank out of your eye, and then you will see clearly to remove the speck in your brother's eye?"' (Luke 6:41–42). He is saying that we are qualified to judge when the plank in our eye is gone! And if we think it is gone, we are deceived.

Pragmatic reasons for not judging others

Why did Jesus give these words, '"Do not judge, and you will not be judged"'? First, He does not want us to grieve the Holy Spirit. Pointing the finger always does this. Second, He wants to help us in all our relationships. Love 'keeps no records of wrongs'

(1 Corinthians 13:5). Why do we keep records? To show that we have paid what was due. A husband will say to his wife, 'I will remember that' – and he does, quoting back some comment she made days before. This is done not to build her up but to put her down. Judging – pointing the finger – is a common ingredient in marriage break-down. But it is what will make one unpopular anywhere – in the office, at church, on campus or anywhere else.

Jesus also gave us this command not to judge because it will spare us of being judged. Who likes being judged? It hurts when someone points the finger at you – whether or not what they say is true. But Luke 6:37 comes with a promise: the best way to avoid being judged is not to judge! The best way to avoid criticism is to stop pointing the finger. When you judge another you put their backs up; they are going to get verbal revenge one way or the other!

And yet there is still another reason we should not judge. It is playing God. Only He has the right to judge. We are elbowing in on His territory when we judge. If you and I engage in pointing the finger, we should remember that God is listening and that He knows the truth about us! He knows what we have thought, done and said. But this makes me think of Ecclesiastes 7:21: 'Do not pay attention to every word people say, or you may hear your servant cursing you – for you know in your heart that many times you yourself have cursed others.'

God's justice is absolutely fair. What is more, He will see that you and I are judged when we do the judging. Every word will be accounted for. Are we prepared to be judged? 'In the same way', then, we 'will be judged' (Matthew 7:2). For example, when I judge you for what I have myself done, God knows this full well. I will be judged according to the way I judge. The standard of measure I choose will be applied to me. I could decide to withhold judgment and choose mercy – which means I can avoid being criticised. Or if I decide to throw the book at you, you may be sure I will get it back. At work here is not only human nature but God himself stepping in. If we get away with pointing the finger, it is not a good sign. Why? God chastens those He loves (see Hebrews 12:6 KJV). If you manage to get away with pointing the finger, it suggests He is not on your case, but when you don't get away with judging, it is a sign God loves you and is preparing you for what is coming around the corner.

How God is at work behind the scenes

God's sense of fair play lies behind our pointing the finger. It is the principle of sowing and reaping. If we show mercy, we will be given mercy; if we choose to judge, we will be judged. You and I determine how it will be. Remember too that God loves to take the side of the underdog. He blesses those who are for the underdog and judges those who neglect the underdog. So when you and I judge another, or even are judged by someone, remember Paul: 'You, then, why do you judge your brother? Or why do you look down on your brother? For we will all stand before God's judgment seat' (Romans 14:10).

It is our pride that makes us want to play God. Don't do that; don't judge. But once you realise you have done this, fall on your knees and ask for mercy. The shrewdest thing you can do is to judge yourself. Paul promised, '... if we judged ourselves, we would not come under judgment' (1 Corinthians 11:31).

And yet Paul says he does not judge himself. So how do we reconcile 1 Corinthians 11:31, which tells us to judge ourselves, and 1 Corinthians 4:3, where Paul says he does not even judge himself? The answer is that in 1 Corinthians 11:31 – in the context of being judged for abusing the Lord's Supper – Paul is telling us how to prevent God stepping in and judging us, as in our being ill, weak or taken on home to heaven. In 1 Corinthians 4:3, Paul was being judged by injudicious Corinthians. In that context he makes the claim that he has not bothered to judge himself so as to vindicate his honour. Although he says he does not know anything against himself, that does not make him innocent. He is prepared for the Supreme Judge to do the open vindicating – in his time. '... wait till the Lord comes. He will bring to light what is hidden in darkness and will expose the motives of men's hearts. At that time each will receive his praise from God' (1 Corinthians 4:5).

That 'praise from God' is the very same thing as the praise that is promised in John 5:44 ('praise that comes from the only God') to which I referred in the previous chapter. This is the praise that comes from God because you diligently sought it rather than the praise of people.

Principle of vindication

It is pride, then, that makes us judge; it is pride that seeks to vindicate ourselves. The Apostle Paul had made a huge step forward in this area: he refused to clear his name and simply chose to wait for the day God chooses to do it.

How will God clear our name? It might be in this life. It might await the Final Judgment. It is best not to look for vindication in this life. This is why you should say with Paul, 'I do not even judge myself' (1 Corinthians 4:3). Don't vindicate yourself in your own eyes. Just let all judging be in suspension until God decides to step in. Yes, He may clear your name in the here and now. I have known Him to do this. But He might let you wait indefinitely – and postpone your vindication until the Judgment Seat of Christ. Can you live with this? You and I must be willing to wait until the Final Day – and live throughout our earthly journey without the vindication that our flesh yearns for. Our vindication should be like that of Jesus – by the Spirit (1 Timothy 3:16). This means you are conscious of God's approval. And if you have that, you are in the best possible state!

Try loving them

My suggestion to you: try loving them rather than judging them. 'There is no fear in love' (1 John 4:18). This way you will 'keep no record of wrongs'. Love 'does not boast' (1 Corinthians 13:4–5). You will not point the finger. If you are judging all the time, then the idea of loving them will not even cross your mind. It is an awful way to live – waiting for the chance to play 'Gottcha!' Don't go there. Love them instead. This gives God great pleasure, honour and glory.

An adequate sense of sin is perhaps the best remedy against judging others. When you see your own depravity and wicked motives – and you remember what you have been forgiven of – it should cause you and me to lower our voices and stop pointing the finger. When I stop and think of the things God has forgiven me of – and the things I got away with – I am so humbled.

In my quiet time this morning it came to me for some reason to thank God for people who have been a blessing to me since I was a child. I mentioned quite a number of people who have been a blessing, who have been influential and pivotal in my life. I began to feel ashamed I had not properly thanked God for them before. I only tried to make up for it – in a small measure. But there is more (not all of my quiet times are like this); I began to reflect on how deep and wide God's forgiveness has been. It is not for you to know how unworthy I am. I can only tell you that if you knew how gracious God has been to me – what He has forgiven me of over these many years – you would only conclude with me: if God can use me, he can use anybody.

In a word: I have no excuse for the pride that would make me point the finger at you – or anybody. When I hear of someone falling, I say, 'Except for the sheer grace of God, that's me'. When I hear of someone who has failed, I say, 'Except for the sheer grace of God, that's me'. When I see another judging unfairly, pointing the finger, throwing the book at someone or bringing up another's past so ruthlessly, I say, 'Except for the sheer grace of God, that's me'. When it comes to being judgmental I sometimes fear I am the world's worst.

Could I remind you of the purpose of this book? It is to help us come to terms with our pride and to make us want to do something about it. I will not let this book close until we observe ways in which we might overcome pride. But may we never – ever – forget the pit from which we have been dug. Learn of yourself what Martin Luther learned about himself: he became afraid of his own heart. Does this surprise you? Yes, no doubt you can take this too far. But if you are aware of your heart's capabilities you will say the same thing as Luther did.

When Jesus said that '"the flesh profiteth"' (KJV) or '"counts for nothing"' (John 6:63), he was saying what Paul later said, 'I know that nothing good lives in me, that is, in my sinful nature' (Romans 7:18). It is a wise and judicious person who learns not to trust the flesh – their motives, their judging us or even our own perception of things. Jeremiah got it right: 'The heart is deceitful ... and desperately wicked; who can know it?' (Jeremiah 17:9 KJV). When you see this is literally true about your own heart, just maybe it will slow you down on judging others.

17

THE GOSPEL

'I am not ashamed of the gospel, because it is the power of God for the salvation of everyone who believes: first for the Jew, then for the Gentle.'

Romans 1:16

'But God chose the foolish things of the world to shame the wise; God chose the weak things of the world to shame the strong. He chose the lowly things of this world and the despised things – and the things that are not – to nullify the things that are, so that no one may boast before him.'

1 Corinthians 1:27–29

'To depend partly on Christ's righteousness and partly upon our own is to set one foot upon a rock and another in the quick sands. Christ will either be to us all in all in points of righteousness, or else nothing at all.'

Thomas Erskine (1750–1823)

'When I was coming to Christ, I thought I was doing it all myself, and although I sought the Lord earnestly, I had no idea the Lord was seeking me ... I saw that God was at the bottom of it all, and that he was the Author of my faith ... I ascribe my change wholly to God ... A sinner can no more repent and believe without the Holy Spirit's aid than he can create a world.'

Charles H. Spurgeon (1834–1892)

It is difficult to say which aspect of the Gospel of Jesus Christ is more offensive: (1) that salvation is totally by grace and not of human effort, (2) that only those who have faith in Christ are saved – and all others lost, or (3) that a wicked person can go throughout his or her life and be saved at the last minute and go to heaven and a moral person can live a clean life to the end and be eternally lost. The reason these propositions – all true – are offensive is due to one word: pride.

We don't like the idea of getting something for nothing. If someone lends a helping hand, we say, 'Can I please pay you for this? Or do something for you?' We struggle with something being completely given to us. A reason for this is that we don't like to be in debt to anybody. If we can pay our way we save face; to be saved by sheer grace is – to some – losing face.

The Gospel of Jesus Christ is designed with basically one thing in mind: that God gets all the glory. That no one 'should glory in his presence' (1 Corinthians 1:29 KJV), that is, 'boast before him' (NIV). God is a 'God of glory' (Acts 7:2). If you take all of God's attributes – His omniscience, omnipresence, omnipotence, wisdom, love, justice – and came up with *one word* that summarises them all, it is His *glory*. Therefore, when we get to heaven, we will be giving Him all the glory that we are there. We will be able to take no credit for our being there. But, as Spurgeon put it, when we first come to the Lord it seems like what we do is in our own strength – 'I thought I was doing it all myself', he said; but later we come to see that God 'was at the bottom of it all'.

How does this make you feel? Are you okay with this? Does this surprise you? I'm sorry, but the 'gospel' that is preached nowadays, speaking generally, is 'no gospel at all' (Galatians 1:7). First, the emphasis seems to be on what *we* do. Second, the emphasis is often on the earthly benefits of becoming a Christian – that is, what it will do for you here below (your finances, healing, well-being). In a word: it is so man-centred. The 'what's in it for me?' era continues to govern our world view.

Paul said he was 'not ashamed of the gospel, because it is the power of God for … *salvation* (Romans 1:16). Had he said the

Gospel was the power of God regarding prosperity or healing, there would have been no need for him to say 'I am not ashamed'. There would be no offence had the Gospel been primarily for our finances or health. But when it is all about Jesus dying on the cross for our sins – which is what Romans is chiefly about – it becomes necessary for one to stand up and be counted: are you ashamed of this Gospel or not? When Paul came to Corinth, he 'resolved to know nothing' among them 'except Jesus Christ and him crucified' (1 Corinthians 2:2). Had he marched into Corinth with a gospel of healing or financial prosperity, the people there would have lined up for miles to get in on it. No offence would have been involved. But when Paul mentioned Jesus Christ and Him crucified, you could almost say he was putting Christianity's most offensive aspect before them; for there would be nothing appealing about this to the Greek mind. And yet Paul knew the only way people could be saved was through the cross of Christ; he therefore plunged in at the deep end from the start!

We are talking, therefore, about a Gospel that gives God all the glory and men and women *no* glory. There is not a thing about the Gospel that allows man to boast. He can't take credit for choosing God: God chose him (2 Timothy 1:9). He can't take credit for believing this Gospel: faith is a gift of God (Ephesians 2:8). He can't take credit for his good works and holy life that got him to heaven: we are saved by grace and 'not by works, so that no one can boast' (Ephesians 2:9). He can't claim he is saved by his righteousness: God's righteousness has been imputed to us – 'his faith is credited as righteousness' (Romans 4:5). So Paul raised a question: 'Where, then, is boasting?' and then gave the answer: 'It is excluded' (Romans 3:27). In summary: God removed all ground for boasting right from the beginning!

When God provided a Saviour, it meant He came down to this earth Himself. Yes, Jesus was God. 'In the beginning was the Word, and the Word was with God, and the Word was God' (John 1:1). And yet – 'The Word became flesh and lived for a while among us (John 1:14). Jesus was God as though He were not man; He was man as though He were not God. He was and is the God-man – and will be for ever and ever, throughout eternity.

When Jesus died on the cross, here is what happened. First, he fulfilled the Mosaic Law. The most stupendous claim Jesus ever made, reckoned Dr Martyn Lloyd-Jones, was when Jesus said he had come '"to fulfil the Law"' (Matthew 5:17). Nobody in human history had ever made such a claim. It was Jesus' way of saying He would keep the Law – all 2,000 pieces of Mosaic legislation – by his personal life. This means He kept the Civil Law (how people should govern themselves), the Ceremonial Law (how God should be worshipped), and the Moral Law (the Ten Commandments). This is why He came to the earth.

He fulfilled the Law in two ways: by His sinless life and sacrificial death. His death was the fulfilment of all the sacrificial system that was introduced by the Law of Moses. The Mosaic Law was a temporary measure from the beginning; it was never meant to be permanent. You could call it a parenthesis – brackets – that lasted from about 1300 BC until AD 33 when Jesus died on the cross. Just before He died, Jesus uttered the words 'it is finished' (John 19:30), the translation of the Greek word *tetelestai* which was a colloquial expression in the ancient market place that meant 'paid in full'. In a word: Jesus paid our debt on the cross. The debt we owe to God – a sinless life – Jesus offered on our behalf.

Believing the Gospel, then, means submitting to the Saviour's substitutionary work. He took our place. He was our substitute. We are saved by transferring the trust we had in our good works to what Jesus did for us on the cross. We do this transferring by the help of the Holy Spirit. We are therefore saved by God's effectual calling through the Holy Spirit and by Jesus' death on the cross.

The blood of Jesus does two things: expiation and propitiation. Expiation – sometimes called atonement – is what the blood does for *us*: it washes away our sins. Propitiation – sometimes called satisfaction – is what the blood does for *God*: it turns away His wrath from us because the blood of His Son *satisfies His justice*. Charles Spurgeon said there is no Gospel apart from substitution and satisfaction. Substitution refers to the fact the Jesus was literally doing everything in our behalf – by his keeping the Law for us and dying for us. This is why we 'put all our eggs into one basket': Jesus and His death. Satisfaction means that God's justice has been completely and eternally satisfied by what Jesus did for us when He shed His blood.

Tell me, how can you and I take any credit for this? We can't. What happens to our pride? It is gone, gone, *gone*, GONE!

> 'Not the labour of my hands
> Can fulfil Thy law's demands;
> Could my zeal no respite know,
> Could my tears forever flow,
> All for sin could not atone:
> Thou must save, and Thou alone.
>
> Nothing in my hand I bring,
> Simply to Thy cross I cling; ...'
>
> Augustus Toplady (1740–78)

It is humbling. It means totally swallowing our pride. All we can do is bow and sing, ' "Worthy is the Lamb, who was slain, to receive power and wealth and wisdom and strength and honour and glory and praise!" ' (Revelation 5:12).

Our first reaction to the Gospel is often negative, especially the part that salvation is totally by grace and not by our works. But when we submit to this truth, it becomes sweeter as the days go by. You wouldn't want it any other way!

But remember too: 'You are not your own; you are bought at a price. Therefore honour God with your body' (1 Corinthians 6:19–20). This means that God trusts us with the responsibility 'to live lives worthy of God' (1 Thessalonians 2:12) and the Gospel. Near the end of his magnificent letter to the Romans, Paul put an important 'therefore' – which applies to all who adore the Gospel he has outlined: 'Therefore, I urge you, brothers, in view of God's mercy, to offer your bodies as living sacrifices, holy and pleasing to God – which is your spiritual worship' (Romans 12:1). Living sanctified lives is a way of saying 'Thank you' to God for so great a salvation. And what about being in debt to someone because they have been so kind? Said Paul: 'I am under obligation ...' (Romans 1:14 ESV), 'I am debtor ...' (KJV). We will be debtors as long as we live.

> When I survey the wondrous cross
> On which the Prince of glory died,
> My richest gain I count but loss,
> And pour contempt on all my pride.
>
> Were the whole realm of nature mine,
> That were a present far too small!
> Love so amazing, so divine,
> Demands my soul, my life, my all.
>
> Isaac Watts (1674–1748)

Paul was not ashamed of this Gospel. Are you? Surely not! But if you have not embraced it, I urge you to pray this prayer *now* – wherever you are:

> Lord Jesus Christ, I need you. I want you. I am sorry for my sins. Wash my sins away by your blood. I know I cannot save myself. I transfer my trust in my good works to what you did for me on the cross. I welcome your Holy Spirit into my heart. As best as I know how, I give you my life. Amen.

If you prayed that prayer, share it! Tell at least one other person today. From this day forward pray daily. Read your Bible daily. Witness for Christ daily. Remember your life has changed. You are not your own. Find a church where the Bible is preached, where Christ is honoured and the Holy Spirit is welcomed. And always live so that you will not be ashamed to share Jesus Christ wherever you are. Don't let your pride interfere!

18

OVERCOMING PRIDE

'The Christian life is not a constant high. I have moments of deep discouragement. I have to go to God in prayer with tears in my eyes, and say, "O God, forgive me," or "Help me."'
   Billy Graham (b. 1918)

'I didn't go to religion to make me happy. I always knew a bottle of Port would do that. If you want a religion to make you really feel comfortable, I certainly don't recommend Christianity.'
   C. S. Lewis (1898–1963)

'If we claim to be without sin, we deceive ourselves and the truth is not in us. If we confess our sins, he is faithful and just and will forgive us our sins and purify us from all unrighteousness.'
   1 John 1:8–9

'We must all appear before the judgment seat of Christ, that each one may receive what is due to him for the things done while in the body, whether good or bad.'
   2 Corinthians 5:10

No great claim to overcome pride completely is pretended in this, our final chapter. We begin by knowing that we are sinners, that we will always be imperfect in this life – no matter how long and hard we try to be otherwise.

Then why try? I answer: because we are debtors to the great and glorious Gospel. All attempts to please God not only honour him but result in *some* progress on our way to heaven. I would hate to think what I would be like had I not resolved a long time ago to walk in all the light God gives me and to aim for perfection. I doubt not that I would not only be a thousand times worse off, but that I would also have been shipwrecked years ago. But what I can promise – indeed, guarantee – is that by heeding Holy Scripture, we can improve and spare ourselves a lot of trouble down the road. We are far, far better off to make every attempt to overcome pride than to say, 'What's the use?'

Today (as it happens) is my seventy-fifth birthday. I take comfort from knowing that Abraham's life was ahead of him when he was seventy-five (see Genesis 12:4). Although I do not expect to live as long as he did, I have a future hope that is equal to the way I felt over fifty years ago. And what if I die tomorrow? I will thank God for giving me these years in which I have sought to honour Him who has been infinitely gracious to me. I sometimes wonder if ever – *ever* – a child of God was as unworthy as I. So: here follows my best wisdom on how to overcome pride.

Admit that you are proud

You will make no progress in overcoming pride as long as you deny that it exists in you. It is there. You know it is. Not all of it – like cholesterol, as we saw in Chapter 2 – is bad. But too much of it is, and we must do all we can to make improvements in our spiritual health. So, admit that you are a proud person. When you get hurt by someone, do not resent it. It may well be that your pride is wounded and that they are insensitive. But admit that your pride has been injured. Don't tell *them*; tell God. 'I poured out my complaint before him; I shewed before him my trouble' (Psalms 142:2 kjv).

God likes your company. He loves it when you confide in Him. This means you confide in Him alone; don't tell all your secrets to the people around you. Who knows, God may show you things you never dreamed of (see Psalm 25:14). Talk to Him. Spend time with Him. There will be no praying in heaven. He loves your wanting to be near Him.

Share all your feelings with Him. Your envy. Pride. Jealousies. Hurts. Don't worry, He can cope! He welcomes you to confide in Him. Do not be surprised if He begins to confide in you as well. You may well discover sooner than later that all which has happened to you was God's way of trying to get your attention so you would spend more time with Him.

Never forget good old 1 John 1:9 (you can't wear it out): 'If we confess our sins [God] is faithful and just and will forgive us our sins and purify us from all unrighteousness.' That verse is for you and me. It is a reminder why Jesus died for us.

Don't justify it

This book will have failed you if by this time you are still making excuses for your pride – as if you were exceptional. Or that your hurt was so great that your anger was justified. Wrong. Your temper may get you into trouble, but pride keeps you angry. It is a big mistake to justify your pride. Don't say, 'It's in my genes, my parents were like this, my relatives are like this'.

I reply: your *first* parents were like this – Adam and Eve. Their sin passed on a sinful nature into which you were born. Pride was born in the heavens when Lucifer wanted to be like God (Isaiah 14:13–14). This became Eve's problem when she partook of the forbidden fruit (Genesis 3:6a). Then Adam partook and both were ashamed (Genesis 3:6b–7). God asked Adam what was going on. As I said above, Adam blamed Eve, Eve blamed the serpent. And passing the buck has been going on ever since.

When we justify our pride, we will remain in the same mess. But if we own it as something that is sinful, then confess it, we are on our way toward recovery.

Resist temptations to pride

We all need to anticipate temptation. The temptation that challenges your pride will be at the top of the list. Learn to recognise how close pride is to your temptation. The sooner you recognise how *pride* is at the bottom of your temptations, the better you will be equipped to resist.

The temptation to boast. This can be subtle. Love – selfless concern – 'does not boast' (1 Corinthians 13:4). This is because the love of God in our hearts is fulfilling in itself, so there is no need to boast. But when you are tempted to name-drop, ask yourself: is it going to make them feel better or me feel better if I tell where I have been yesterday, or who I was with this week, or where I am invited to be this week-end? In a word: does it bless them? If in your heart of hearts you know it is doing more for your ego than for than for their benefit, bite your tongue! You will only be sorry you told what you know. 'When boasting ends, there dignity begins.'

The temptation to hold a grudge. The problem with grudges and unforgiveness is that it always seems right – at first. 'If you only knew what they did, you'd be bitter too', you may say. And I would almost certainly agree with you. Since I wrote the book *Total Forgiveness*, I have been sent many testimonies of people who have been deeply hurt. Almost all of these have been wounded far more than I. I feel that what we went through at Westminster Chapel was a drop in the bucket when compared to the sorrow, heartaches, betrayal, wickedness and injustices some people have had to overcome. But the stories how they overcame are so wonderful!

Holding a grudge always seems right but is always wrong. I promise: you will not die by swallowing your pride. The thing is, it hurts our pride to forgive! 'They don't deserve it.' Quite. But wait a minute. Do you deserve being forgiven? I answer: give that rogue a gift he or she doesn't deserve – forgive them. Totally. And who gets the benefit? Them? Perhaps. But absolutely and certainly *you* do. I guarantee it.

Medical people have discovered how holding a grudge is injurious to your health, that it can cause high blood pressure, arthritis, kidney disease, heart disease. They have also found that the benefit of forgiveness is not so much to the one who gets forgiven; the benefit comes to the one who *does the forgiving*! And yet another reason for forgiveness can be summed up: to keep from being 'outsmarted' by Satan (see 2 Corinthians 2:11 NLT).

When you hold a grudge, although you certainly didn't mean to, the moment you withhold forgiveness. You give the devil access to you. He will take full advantage of it, I'm afraid. Don't give him this pleasure.

What happens is this. The moment we refuse to forgive, the devil will ride on top of that bitterness to make us grieve the Holy Spirit. When we grieve the Holy Spirit we lose presence of mind, clear thinking and the sense of God's presence. If this sin is not dealt with in a short period of time, the devil will get us set in our ways – making it harder and harder to forgive. We dig our heels in, feel justified and – if we aren't careful – become unteachable.

Give the person who has hurt you a gift they don't deserve: total forgiveness – and notice how the peace returns to your heart. You will even feel better! It gives your pride a severe blow and it means a major victory for you.

The temptation to judge. Pointing the finger is the easiest thing in the world to do. As I said above, I fear that my greatest weakness is this – judging people. For we, who don't suffer fools gladly, become very smug and self-righteous. We fancy we are a cut above them. We look down on them, put them in their place. This is never right to do.

Resisting the temptation to judge is not easy. But it works! Refuse to say what comes to your mind. Remember the fringe benefit of not judging: you don't get judged! In other words, not only do you keep from grieving the Holy Spirit, you make life easier for everybody.

The temptation to save face. In Dale Carnegie's book *How to Win Friends and Influence People* – a book I read many years ago – he says that we should let the other person 'save face'. He reckons we win a friend for life if we let them save face. This means we not only protect their fragile ego, but do it in such a way that we 'cover' for them, that is, we behave as though they didn't even do anything wrong (although we know they did). It is the way Joseph treated his brothers who had been so wicked. He could say to them in so many words, '... God meant it for good' (see Genesis 45:8, 50:20 ESV). Instead of 'rubbing their noses in it', we overlook it entirely.

God always lets us save face. He will never tell what we did. Our sins are buried. They are forgotten. God never throws up our past. We all have skeletons in the closet. God is not waiting for a chance to yank out that skeleton and show it to the world. No. He protects us, lets us save face. Although it is not a Christian book, I think all Christians – especially those in leadership – should read *How to Win Friends and Influence People*.

There is more; to resist the temptation to save face may sometimes even mean the willingness to lose face. Yes. When Paul reminded the Corinthians that '[Christ] was crucified in weakness' (2 Corinthians 13:4), he set himself up to be like Jesus on the cross. These people were accusing Paul unjustly. But Paul was prepared to look like a wimp. That is not easy to do. But Jesus was that – appearing to be so weak and helpless. Think about it: He who is the Creator of the universe and could have called 10,000 angels to deliver Him from being crucified, instead submitted to the Jews, the chief priest, Herod and Pilate. It was so humiliating for Him. But He did it not for Himself but for us.

Yes, you and I are called to do this from time to time. Instead of showing how strong, courageous and powerful we are, we willingly lose face – and appear to be weaklings. But the benefit is tremendous – the presence of God will flood your soul, you will be given a wonderful peace and joy. Last but not least, you have a major victory over pride.

The temptation to focus on compliments. Caution: never 'fish' for a compliment. Don't go seeking compliments, don't even go looking for them. This will become an addiction. You may or may not face my own temptations in this area. When I have preached and fear I have not done well I hope, hope, *hope* someone will compliment my sermon! They may or may not. The temptation is to say something that will motivate them to comment one way or the other. I've done it – was always sorry for doing so. I have had to come to the place I *refuse* to say a word that will cause a person to comment on my sermon. Why? I want the honour and praise that comes from *God*. If I manage to get a positive word from someone who heard me, God virtually says, 'Okay, R.T., you wanted their compliment and their compliment you got – are you happy?' I have had that happen. And I feel horrible because I just showed that their compliment meant more to me than waiting to see what God might convey later in His own way.

This does not mean we don't appreciate compliments. We never outgrow the appreciation for a kind, gracious and affirming word from people. But if this comes because we encourage it, we reveal how much it meant – far more, sadly, than God's praise. But if, on the other hand, you want God's praise more than anything else, there may come from people – with God's permission – a compliment because we did not encourage it.

In a word: learn not to take compliments too seriously. Arthur Blessitt once said to me, 'When you can accept praise or criticism equally, you are beginning to get free'.

The Judgment Seat of Christ

I have referred to the Final Judgment more than once in this book. For a full treatment see my book *Judgment Seat of Christ*. In summary:

The Final Judgment will be in two parts – (1) who is in and who is out regarding going to heaven; the saved go to heaven, the lost go to hell. The only way we get to heaven is by trusting not our good works but only in Jesus Christ, whose blood satisfied the justice of God. That is salvation.

However, there is (2) a judgment among the *saved*. This determines whether the Christian receives a 'reward' at the Judgment Seat of Christ. The judgment will be based upon the quality of our superstructure. There is the foundation (salvation – 1 Corinthians 3:11) and the superstructure (basis for reward – 1 Corinthians 3:12). Here is the teaching summed up: all who are on the foundation go to heaven, but not all built a lasting superstructure; in other words, not all who go to heaven will receive a reward at the Judgment Seat of Christ. The superstructure is determined by such things as our forgiving others, walking in the light God gives us and seeking His honour and not the praise of men. If the superstructure is comprised of gold, silver, precious gems – things that will not burn – then we will receive a reward. For the Day will be revealed by fire. But should our superstructure be made up of wood, hay, straw – things that will burn when the fire is revealed – we lose our reward (see 1 Corinthians 3:10–15).

Our pride is pivotal in whether we receive a reward at the Final Judgment. If we choose to protect our egos, remain smug and point the finger at others, we erect a superstructure that will be burnt up on the Day of Judgment.

You may say: 'I don't care whether I receive a reward, I just want to make it to heaven – that's good enough for me'. I reply: a spiritual person does not speak or think like that. A reward was of high importance for Paul (see 1 Corinthians 9:25–27). I myself want a reward. What is the reward? It consists partly of taking off our crowns and casting them at the feet of Jesus. If we have no crown – reward – we will feel horrible on that day: it means you will have no crown to lay at His feet. That's not all; we should all want to 'receive a rich welcome' (2 Peter 1:11) on that Day. I want to hear Jesus say, 'Well done'. Don't you?

My pride, then, is a determining factor with reference to that reward. We can overcome pride by looking forward to that Day when we hear Jesus say to us, 'Well done. Good'. You see, every idle word will be remembered on that Day (see Matthew 12:36). It is pride which lies behind almost all our words. The truth of what we really are – how clever, what we know, the truth regarding our motivation and godly walk – will be unveiled that day. If you and I are truly governed by the Judgment Seat of Christ, it will totally change our lives now.

Embrace the Gospel

The Gospel is the greatest remedy against pride. This is because it is so humbling to receive a gift – absolutely free. God has done it all. He has provided the Saviour who lived the perfect life. He grants us the repentance and faith that secures our salvation. We can take no credit for any of it!

So embrace this Gospel. Stand for it. Uphold it. Talk about it. Learn to present it to others. And show you are unashamed of it. This will help you to overcome pride!

I died a thousand deaths when God called me to begin the Pilot Light ministry at Westminster Chapel. Here I was, out in Buckingham Gate (the street between Westminster Chapel and Buckingham Palace – talking to passers-by, strangers, tourists, tramps and, now and then, middle class people. It was far easier to remain in the pulpit – speaking to thousands than to one other person. It really hurt my pride. But I got over it. It changed my life.

You may not have to do that. But if you are true to the leading of the Holy Spirit, you will have to do things that humble you, make you appear as a wimp and do things that nobody will admire. And yet it is a major step in overcoming pride.

At the end of the day it comes down to the Gospel. Embrace it with both hands. And never look back.

CONCLUSION

I will never forget the last time I visited with Dr John Stott, the Rector Emeritus of All Soul's Church in London. I made it a point to visit him as often as I could. But for some reason he said something to me that I wasn't expecting. Knowing him as I do, he would want me to share it here. He said, 'If you really knew me, you would spit in my face'.

I can hardly recall that moment without coming to tears. I think those who know John Stott would agree that he was one of the meekest, humblest men on the planet. But that is what he said. A proud man could not speak like that.

We are all sinners. We all fight to overcome pride.

The hymnwriters John Newton and William Cowper were close friends. One morning, reflecting upon the words, '... by the grace of God I am what I am ...' (1 Corinthians 15:10), John Newton looked across the kitchen table and said to William Cowper: 'I'm not what I ought to be. I'm not what I want to be. I'm not what I hope to be. But thank God I'm not what I used to be.'

The problem with pride is that we can slip, fall and seem too much like we used to be. But if this book can serve to convict one of sin and motivate us to be more like Jesus – even if by inches rather than miles, perhaps it will have done some good. May the blessing of God Almighty – Father, Son and Holy Spirit – be with you, dear reader, now and ever more. Amen.